The March of Destiny

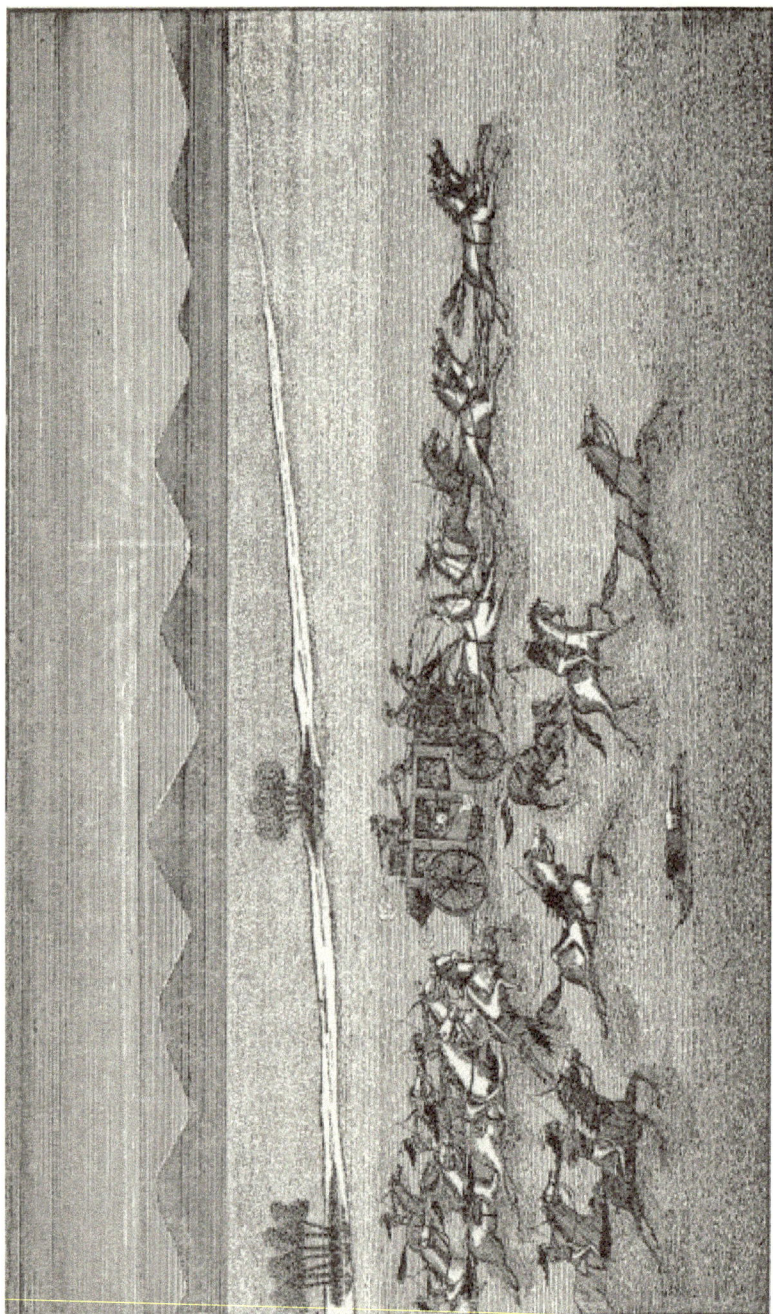

The March of Destiny

Two Accounts of Early Emigrants to Colorado

Dangers of the Trail in 1865
by Charles E. Young
★

The Story of a Pioneer
by V. Divinny

LEONAUR

The March of Destiny: Two Accounts of Early Emigrants to Colorado
Dangers of the Trail in 1865 by Charles E. Young
The Story of a Pioneer by V. Devinny

Leonaur is an imprint of Oakpast Ltd

Material original to this edition and this editorial selection
copyright © 2009 Oakpast Ltd

ISBN: 978-1-84677-748-6 (hardcover)
ISBN: 978-1-84677-747-9 (softcover)

http://www.leonaur.com

Publisher's Notes

The views expressed in this book are not necessarily
those of the publisher.

Contents

THE STORY OF A PIONEER

Dangers of the Trail

Preface

I present this narrative of actual events on a trip across the plains to Denver, Colorado, in 1865 and of life in the Far West in the later sixties.

An interesting and valuable feature is a map of the country, made in 1865, by Henry Bowles of Boston, showing the old Platte River and Smoky Hill Trails of that day before there was a railroad west of the Missouri River.

Everything is told in a plain but truthful manner, and this little volume is submitted to the reader for approval or criticism.

Chas. E. Young
July, 1912

Chapter 1

Young Man, Go West

Early in 1859 gold was discovered in Colorado, and Horace Greeley, the well known writer and a power throughout the country both before and during the Civil War, made, in the interest of the *New York Tribune*, of which he was editor, an overland trip to Denver by the first stage line run in that day. He started from Leavenworth, Kansas, and with the exception of Mr. Richardson, of the *Boston Journal*, was the only passenger in the coach. The trip was not all that could be desired, for they met with numerous hardships and many narrow escapes, as did hundreds of others who had preceded them over that dangerous trail, many never reaching their destination—having met death at the hands of the cruel Indians of the plains.

During his stay in Denver Mr. Greeley wrote a number of letters to the *New York Tribune*, confirming the finding of gold in the territory and advising immigration. The people in the East were sceptical in regard to its discovery and awaited a written statement from him to this effect.

At the close of the war Mr. Greeley's advice to young

men, through the columns of his paper, was to go West and grow up with the country, and it became a byword throughout the State of New York and the Nation, "Young man, go West and grow up with the country."

Could Mr. Greeley have foreseen the number of young lives that were to be sacrificed through his advice, I think he would have hesitated before giving it; yet, it was the most valued utterance of any public man of that day for the settlement of the then Far West.

After reading a number of these letters in the *New York Tribune*, I became very enthusiastic over the opportunities that the West offered for the young man. There was also a loyal friend of mine who became as enthusiastic over it as myself. Thus, while we were still so young as to be called boys, we made up our minds to follow Mr. Greeley's advice, and "Go West and grow up with the country."

In making our purchases for the trip we were obliged to make our plans known to an acquaintance, who at once expressed a desire to accompany us. After consultation, we consented and at the appointed time, the fore part of July, 1865, just at the close of the Civil War, we boarded a New York Central train at the depot in Geneva, N.Y., with no thought of the hardships and dangers we would be called upon to meet. The first night found us at the Falls of Niagara—the most stupendous production of nature that the country was known to possess at that time. Our time was divided between the American and Canadian sides, viewing the grand spectacle at all hours, from the rising to the setting of the sun; and, awed by the marvellous masterpiece of grandeur, we were held as if fascinated by its beauty, until we were forced to leave for the want of food and to replenish our commissary. When we boarded the cars to be whirled through the then wilds of Lower Canada, we were liberally supplied with the best the country produced.

MAP OF TRAILS LEADING FROM MISSOURI RIVER TO DENVER, COLORADO 1865

Upon the fifth day we rolled into Chicago, the cosmopolitan city of the West. Two days later we reached Quincy, Ill., where we made connection with the old Hannibal & St. Joe Railroad which was to take us through Missouri to Atchison, Kansas. Missouri, after the war, was not an ideal state for a law abiding citizen, much less for inexperienced youths of our age, and we quickly realized that fact. Many stations had their quota of what was termed the Missouri bushwhacker, or, more plainly speaking, outlaws, who, during the war and for some time after, pillaged the state and surrounding country, leaving in their wake death and destruction. They had belonged to neither side at war, but were a set of villains banded together to plunder, burn, ravage and murder young and old alike; as wicked a set of villains as the world has ever known. At many stations they would nearly fill the car, making it very unpleasant for the passengers. Their language and insults caused every one to be guarded in conversation. The condition of the road, however, often gave us relief, as we were obliged to alight and walk, at times, when arriving at a point where ties or rails had to be replaced. Its entire length showed the carnage and destruction of war, making travel slow and dangerous as well as uncomfortable. On reaching the state of bleeding Kansas and the then village of Atchison we were about used up. We at once called at the Ben Holiday Stage Office and inquired the price of a ticket to Denver, but finding it to be beyond our means, we decided to go by ox conveyance.

COMANCHE BILL

We were not long in finding what, in those days, was called a tavern, located in the outskirts of the town. Having been chosen spokesman, I stepped up to the rough board counter and registered. We were soon confronted by the toughest individual we had yet seen. I pleasantly bade him good morning but received no immediate recognition, save a wild stare from two horrible, bloodshot eyes. I quickly came to the conclusion that we were up against the real Western article, nor was I mistaken. He didn't keep up waiting long, for he soon roared out an oath and wanted to know where we were from. After telling him as near as I possibly could, under the circumstances, he again became silent. His look and brace of revolvers were not reassuring, to say the least. He soon came out of his trance and did not keep us long in suspense, for his next act was to pull out both of his life-takers, and, not in very choice language, introduce himself as Comanche Bill from Arkansas, emphasizing the Arkansas by letting the contents of both of his instruments of death pierce the ceiling of his story and a half shack. I have wondered many times since that I am alive. We had been told by a fellow passenger that Atchison was a little short of Hades, and we were fast realizing that our informer was not far out of the way; yet, it was a haven in comparison to other places at which we were yet to arrive. Comanche William, or whatever his right name might have been, was a different person after his forceful introduction.

He began to question me. He asked me if we had any money.

"Yes."

"Any friends?"

"Certainly."

"Well, then you had better get straight back to them, for if you remain in these parts long, they will be unable to recognize you. Where are you fellows headed for, anyway?"

"Denver, Colorado."

"By stage?"

"No, sir. By ox or mule conveyance."

"You are too light weight. No freighter will hire you."

"They will or we'll walk."

"You will not walk far for the Indians along the Platte are ugly. By the way, do you pards ever take anything?"

Not wishing to offend such a character, I gave my companions the wink and we followed him into the bar-room with the full determination of making a friend of him. After all had done the sociable act—of course gentlemen only drink for sociability sake—I took him to one side purposely to draw him into a little private chat, and it was not long before his self-conceit had the better of him. He ordered grub—as all meals were called in the West in those days—for four, stating he was in need of a bite himself. Before the meal had been finished, I became convinced that the old fellow had a tender spot in his makeup, like all tough outlaws, and, if one had tact enough to discover it, he might have great influence over him; otherwise, we would be obliged to sleep with both eyes open and each with his right hand on the butt of his revolver.

THE AMERICAN INDIAN

The following day was passed in taking in the town and Indian Reservation, which was but a short distance from the place. There we came, for the first time, face to face with the American Indian, the sole owner of this vast and fertile continent before the paleface landed to dispute his right of ownership. Foot by foot they had been driven from East, North and South, until at that time they were nearly all west of the great Missouri River, or River of Mud, as the Indians called it. At the suggestion of our landlord, we took with us an interpreter, a few trinkets, and something to moisten the old chief's lips. Upon our arrival we were duly presented to the chief, who invited us to sit on the ground upon fur robes made from the pelts of different animals, including the antelope and the buffalo, or American bison, the monarch of the plains, and each one of us in turn took a pull at the pipe of peace. We then made a tour of their lodges. When we returned, the chief called his squaws to whom we presented our gifts, which pleased them greatly. To the old chief I handed a bottle of Atchison's best. As he grasped it, a smile stole over his ugly face, and with a healthy grunt and a broad grin, he handed me back the empty bottle. Indians love liquor better than they do their squaws. In return he gave me a buffalo robe which later became of great service. After taking another pull at the pipe of peace, we thanked him and took our departure, having no desire to be present when Atchison's invigorator commenced to invigorate his Indian brain.

The impression made by that visit to a supposedly friendly tribe, who at that time had a peace treaty with the government, was not one of confidence. The noble red men, as they were called by the Eastern philanthropist, were as treacherous to the whites as an ocean squall to the navigator. No pen or picture has or can fully describe the cruelty of their nature.

It was dusk when we reached our tavern, and we found it filled with a lawless band of degenerates, as repulsive as any that ever invested Western plains or canyons of the Rockies. We were at once surrounded and by a display of their shooting irons, forced to join in their beastly carnival. It was not for long, however, for a sign from the landlord brought me to his side. He whispered, "When I let my guns loose you fellows pike for the loft." There were no stairs. No sooner had he pulled his life-takers than all the others followed his example. Bullets flew in every direction. Clouds of smoke filled the room, but we had ducked and scaled the ladder to the loft and safety. Sleep was out of the question until the early hours of the morning, for the night was made hideous by blasphemous language, howls of pain and the ring of revolvers. The first call for grub found us ready and much in need of a nerve quieter, which the old sinner laughingly supplied; but no word from him of the night's bloody work. Taking me to one side, he said, "Take no offence, but repeat nothing you hear or see in these parts, and strictly mind your own business and a fellow like you will get into no trouble." I thanked him and followed his advice to the letter during my entire Western life.

The First Camp

After that night's experience, we decided to pay our bill and become acclimated to camp life. We had taken with us a tent, blankets and three toy pistols, the latter entirely useless in that country, which proved how ignorant we were of Western ways. We were not long in finding a suitable camping spot a mile from the town and the same distance from the many corrals of the great Western freighters and pilgrims, as the immigrants were called. For miles we could see those immense, white covered prairie schooners in corral formation. Hundreds of oxen and mules were quietly grazing under the watchful eyes of their herders in saddle. It was certainly a novel sight to the tenderfoot.

We soon had our tent up and leaving one of our number in charge the other two went to town for the necessary camp utensils and grub. Immediately on our return supper was prepared and the novelty enjoyed. After a three days' rest I started out to make the rounds of the corrals in search of a driver's berth. All freighters had a wagon boss and an assistant who rightfully had the reputation of being tyrants when on the trail, using tact and discretion when in camp. A revolver settled all disputes. On approaching them they treated me as well as their rough natures would permit; but I did not take kindly to any of them. They all told me that I was undersized, and too young to stand the dangers and hardships of a trip. I returned to camp much disappointed but not discouraged.

The following morning we proceeded to the large warehouses on the river front, where all Western freighters were to be found. In those days all emigrants and oxen and mule trains with freight going to the far Western Territories would start from either Council Bluffs, Iowa, Leavenworth, Kansas, Atchison or St. Joe, Missouri; Atchison being the nearest point, a large majority embarked from there. The freight was brought up the Missouri River in flat-bottom steam-boats, propelled by a large wheel at the stern, and unloaded on the bank of the river. The perishable goods were placed in the large warehouses but the unperishable were covered with tarpaulin and left where unloaded. They were then transferred to large white covered prairie schooners and shipped to their different points of destination in trains of from twenty-five to one hundred wagons. The rate for freighting depended on the condition of the Indians and ran from ten cents per pound up to enormous charges in some cases.

Securing Passage

After making application to several of the freighters and receiving the same reply as from the wagon bosses, we went a short distance down the river to the last of the warehouses. On our approach we discovered a genuine bullwhacker—as all ox drivers were called in that day—in conversation with a short, stout-built fellow with red hair and whiskers to match. The moment he became disengaged I inquired if he was a freighter. He said that he was and that he wanted more men. His name was Whitehead, just the opposite to the colour of his hair, and as I stepped up to him I wondered what kind of a disposition the combination made—whitehead, redhead. I at once made application for a position for the three of us. In rather a disagreeable voice, he asked me if I could drive. I replied that I could.

"Can you handle a gun and revolver?"

"Certainly."

"How many trips have you made?"

"None."

"Then how the devil do you know you can drive?"

"For the simple reason I am more than anxious to learn, and so are my friends." Then I made a clean breast of the position we were in and urged him to give us a chance.

"Well," he said, "You seem to be a determined little cuss; are the rest of the same timber?"

I told him they were of the same wood but not of the same tree.

After thinking the matter over, he said, "I'll tell you what I will do. I will hire the big fellow for driver at one hundred and twenty-five dollars per month, and the little fellow for night herder at one hundred dollars a month, and yourself for cook for one mess of twenty-five men and for driver in case of sickness or death, at one hundred and twenty-five dollars a month."

We then gave him our names, and, in return, he gave us a note to Mr. Perry, his wagon boss. We at once started for his corral, two miles distant, where we found the gentleman. He asked where our traps were. We told him, and also assured him that we would report for duty the following morning.

When we reached our camp we were completely tired out, but passed the remainder of the day in celebrating our success, and feeling assured that if we escaped the scalping knife of the Indians, we would reach Denver in due time, and, when paid off have a nice sum in dollars.

The following morning we had an early breakfast, broke camp, and reported at the corral where each was presented with two revolvers and a repeating carbine. I was then taken over to the mess wagon which was liberally supplied with bacon (in the rough), flour, beans, cargum (or sour molasses), coffee, salt, pepper, baking-powder and dried apples; the latter we were allowed three times a week for dessert. There was also a skillet for baking bread, which resembled a covered spider without a handle.

When the assistant cook, with whom I was favoured, had started the fire and sufficient coals had accumulated, he would rake them out and place the skillet on them. As soon as the dough was prepared, a chunk was cut off and put in the skillet, the lid placed and covered with coals; in fifteen minutes we would have as nice a looking loaf of bread as one could wish to see, browned to a tempting colour. When eaten warm, it was very palatable, but when cold, only bullwhackers could digest it. An old-fashioned iron kettle in which to stew the beans and boil the dried apples, or vice versa, coffee pots, frying pans, tin plates, cups, iron knives and forks, spoons and a combination dish and bread-pan made up the remainder of the cooking and eating utensils.

Experiences Among the Bushwhackers

It seemed that my assistant was exempt from bringing water, which often had to be carried in kegs for two miles, so he fried the meat and washed the dishes. I soon caught on to the cooking, and doing my best to please everyone, soon became aware of the fact that I had many friends among the toughest individuals on earth, the professional bullwhackers, who, according to their own minds, were very important personages. Their good qualities were few, and consisted of being a sure shot, and expert at lariat and whip-throwing. They would bet a tenderfoot a small sum that they could at a distance of twelve feet, abstract a small piece from his trousers without disturbing the flesh. They could do this trick nine times out of ten. The whips consisted of a hickory stalk two feet long, a lash twelve feet in length with buck or antelope skin snapper nine inches in length. The stalk was held in the left hand, the lash coiled with the right hand and index finger of the left. It was then whirled several times around the head, letting it shoot straight out and bringing it back with a quick jerk. It would strike wherever aimed, raising a dead-head ox nearly off its hind quarters and cutting through the hide and into the flesh. When thrown into space, it would make a report nearly as loud as a revolver. A lariat is a fifty foot line with a running noose at one end and made from the hide of various animals. It is coiled up and carried on the pommel of the saddle. When used for capturing animals or large game, it is whirled several times around the head when the horse is on a dead run and fired at the head of the victim. A professional can place the loop nearly every time.

During the third day of corral life, the steers arrived, and the hard work, mixed with much fun, commenced. A corral is about the shape of an egg, closed by the wagons at one end, and left open to admit the cattle at the other, then closed by chains.

Means of Transportation

Our wheelers and leaders were docile, old freighters, the others were long-horned, wild Texas steers. All of the freighters had their oxen branded for identification, using the first letter of his last name for the purpose. The brand was made from iron and was about four inches in height, attached to a rod three feet in length. A rope was placed over the horns of the animal and his head was drawn tight to the hub of a heavy laden prairie schooner. A bullwhacker, tightly grasping the tail of the beast, would twist him to attention.

The man with the branding implement heated to a white heat would quickly jab the ox on the hind quarter, burning through hair and hide and into the flesh. Then, after applying a solution of salt and water, he was left to recover as best he could. The brand would remain in evidence more than a year unless the steer was captured by cattle thieves, who possessed a secret for growing the hair again in six months. When the branding was completed, each man was given twelve steers to break to yoke, and it was three long weeks before we were in shape to proceed on our long Western tramp. The cattle were driven in each morning at break of day, the same time as when on trail. Each man with a yoke on his left shoulder and a bow in his right hand would go groping about in almost total darkness to select his twelve steers. When they were all found he would yoke them and hitch them to the wagons; the wheelers to the tongue, the leaders in front and the balance to section chains. For days we were obliged to lariat the wildest of them and draw their heads to the hubs of the heavily laden wagons, before being able to adjust the yoke, many times receiving a gentle reminder from the hind hoof of one of the critters to be more careful. I went into the fray with the full determination of learning the profession of driver and at the tenth day I had broken in a team of extras.

On the Sick List

I was then taken sick and for two long weeks kept my bed of earth under the mess wagon, with no mother or doctor, and two thousand miles from home. You may be able to imagine my feelings, but I doubt it. At the end of the second week Mr. Perry came and told me they would make a start the next afternoon and, in his judgment, he thought it unwise to think of making the trip in my present condition. I knew my condition was serious, but I would rather have died on the road, among those outlaws, than to have been left in Atchison among entire strangers. They were all very kind and did what they could for me, but were powerless to check my fast failing strength. I had wasted to less than one hundred pounds in weight and was too weak to even lift an arm.

I pleaded with Mr. Perry for some time and finally overcame his objections. "Well," he said, "Charlie, I will fix a bed in my wagon and you can bunk with me." I objected, for I did not wish to discommode him in the least and told him a good bed could be fixed in the mess wagon. "As you will," he said, and had the boys get some straw which together with the Buffalo robe made a very comfortable bed when not on the move.

A Thunder Storm

The next day they picked me up and put me in the second or reserve mess wagon. Shortly after that the start was made. We had covered less than two miles when all of a sudden I heard the rumbling of distant thunder. Very soon rain began to patter on the canvas covering of my wagon. Then Heaven's artillery broke loose and the water came down in torrents. Never in my young life had I witnessed such a storm. It seemed as if thunder, lightning and clouds had descended to earth and were mad with anger. The racket was deafening. Between the angered claps could be heard the cursing of those Missouri bushwhackers, who, in their oaths, defied the Almighty to do his worst and hurled unspeakable insults at the memory of the mothers who gave them birth. I knew they were trying hard to make corral; whether they could do it, rested entirely with the wagon boss.

The cattle were crazed with fright and the moment they were loose, would certainly stampede. The oxen were finally unyoked and such a snorting and bellowing, it would

Log cabin in Kansas

be impossible to describe. As the racket died away in their mad race, my thoughts turned to my chum, who I knew was with them, and would be trampled beyond recognition by their death-dealing hoofs, if he had not gained his proper position in the rear.

THE LOG CABIN

At that juncture the front flaps of my wagon were parted and at a flash I recognized two of the men, who bore me across the way to the "Old Log Cabin" on the extreme edge of the then Western civilization. As they laid me down I swooned from sheer exhaustion and fright. Before I had become fully conscious I heard that gruff old wagon boss telling the good woman of the cabin to spare nothing for my comfort. She felt of my pulse, asked me a few questions and assured him that she would soon have me on my feet. He bade "God bless me," and passed out into the dark and stormy night. The good woman poked up the fire and placed an old-fashioned, iron tea-kettle in position to do its duty. At that juncture a young miss about my own age came from somewhere, as if by magic, and was told by the good mother to prepare a chicken, that she might make broth for the sick young man, pointing to where I lay. For two hours that good mother worked over me, now and then giving me draughts of hot herb tea, while the daughter deftly prepared nature's wild bird of the prairie, occasionally shooting darts of sympathy from her jet black eyes. When the bird had been cooked, the meat and bones were removed leaving only the broth which was seasoned to a nicety and given me in small quantities and at short intervals until early morning, when I passed into dreamland with the mother keeping vigil as though I were her own son. When I awoke I felt refreshed and comfortable, and found her still at my side, doing for me that which only a mother can.

At daybreak I heard footsteps above; presently the father and son came in. The daughter was called and breakfast was prepared. They told me that our cattle had stampeded and it might be days before they were found. After a three days search my chum and the cattle were overtaken miles from camp, but none the worse for their fearful experience. The moment he arrived he came to see me. I was sitting up for the first time, wrapped in Indian blankets, but very weak. I assured him that I would certainly get well, emphasizing the fact, however, that had we not run into that fearful storm, making my present haven of care possible, I could never have recovered, and believed that the prayers of a loving mother at home had been answered.

A Cattle Stampede

He then related his experience with those storm-maddened cattle. The first clap of thunder awoke him, and when the rain began he knew he was in for a bad night, and had taken every precaution to supply himself with all things needful. His description of the storm and mad race to keep up with those wild animals, crazed with fright, was enough to congeal the blood of a well man, and in my condition it nearly unnerved me. But I was delighted to know that he was safe, for we were like brothers. His safe arrival, together with the motherly care I had received and was receiving, put me rapidly on the gain. Not a morning passed that the daughter did not shoulder her trusty rifle and go out in search of some refreshment for me, always returning with a number of chickens of the prairie. She was a sure shot, as were the entire family, for they were all born and brought up on the border, moving farther West as the country became settled. From the father I learned the treachery of the Indians, their mode of warfare and different methods of attack; in fact, I had the devilish traits of the noble red men—as history called them—down to a nicety.

When the daughter's day's work was done, she would read to me and relate stories of her life, which reminded me of the "Wild Rose" in all its purity and strength.

The fifth day after the cattle were found the train broke corral and proceeded on its long Western tramp. Before leaving, Mr. Perry made arrangements with the old borderman for me to overtake them as soon as I was able.

The fourth day after the train had left, I made up my mind that I would start the next morning at sunrise and so informed my Western friends, whom, I felt, had saved my life. The old borderman expressed regret at my leaving and informed me that both he and his son would accompany me to camp. I thanked him and assured him that I felt a mother could not have done more for her own son than his wife had for me—they had all shown me every consideration possible—and that I should always remember them, which I have. At this juncture the mother spoke up gently, but firmly, and addressing her husband, said, "If you have no objection, daughter will accompany Mr. Young. She is a sure shot, a good horsewoman, and the horses are fleet of foot. We have not heard of any Indians in the neighbourhood for some time, and besides she wants to go and the ride will do her good."

He replied, "My good woman, you cannot tell where the Indians are, they may be miles away today, but here this very night."

"That is true," she said, "but the stage driver told me that he had not seen a redskin since crossing the Nebraska line."

"That may be," he replied, "still they may have been in the bluffs, or sand hills watching their opportunity to surprise one of the many small trains of pilgrims, thinking to overpower them, run off their cattle and massacre all."

THE MARCH OF DESTINY

29

"Yes, that is all true, but I'll wager they could not catch our girl."

After thinking silently for a few moments, he said, "Well, if you wish, she may go; but if anything happens to our little one, you alone will be blamed."

That settled it. We talked long after father and brother had bade us good night. Mother and daughter finally retired; but, as for myself, I was nervous and restless, sleeping little, thinking of home and loved ones; not, however, forgetting the little "Wild Rose" that was separated from me only by a curtain partition.

The following morning we were up at break of day, and at just 5:30 on a lovely August morning the horses were brought to the door and both quickly mounted. Her riding habit of buckskin, trimmed with coloured beads, was the most becoming costume I had ever seen on her during my stay, and for the first time I wished that I were not going, but it was for a moment only.

With the Wagon Train Again

My destination was Denver, and nothing could change my plans except death in the natural way, or being cut down by those treacherous plains roamers. After a pleasant ride which lasted till noon, we came in sight of the corral. When within a quarter of a mile of it, she informed me she was going no farther. Both quickly dismounted. Our conversation would not interest you. Suffice to say, the parting was painful to both. I bade her good-bye and she was off like a flash. I walked slowly into camp, now and then turning to watch the fast retreating figure of as brave a prairie child as nature ever produced. The men appeared glad to see me; the gruff old wagon boss more so than any of the others, for he would not let me turn my hand to any kind of work until I was able. Then I did my best to repay him for his many kindnesses.

At 2 o'clock that afternoon the train broke corral, and for the first time I realized the slowness of our progress, and the long trip before us. Under the most favourable circumstances we could not make over ten miles a day and more often at the beginning three, five and seven.

Our bed was mother earth, a rubber blanket and buffalo robe the mattress, two pairs of blankets the covering, Heaven's canopy the roof; the stars our silent sentinels. The days were warm, the nights cool. We would go into camp at sundown. The cattle were unyoked and driven to water. After grub the night herder and one of the drivers would take them in charge, and if there were no Indians following, would drive them to a good grazing spot over the bluffs.

We passed through Kansas, after crossing the Little and Big Blue rivers, and part of Nebraska without seeing another log cabin or woods. Every fifteen or twenty miles there was a stage station of the Ben Holiday coach line, which ran between Atchison, Kansas, and Sacramento, California. At every station would be a relay of six horses, and by driving night and day would make one hundred miles every twenty-four hours. They were accompanied by a guard of United States soldiers on top of coaches and on horseback.

CHAPTER 2

Arrival at Fort Carney

Arriving at Fort Carney we struck the Platte River trail leading to Denver. We were compelled by United States army officers to halt and await the arrival of a train of fifty armed men before being allowed to proceed. In a few hours the required number came up, together with three wagon loads of pilgrims. No train was permitted to pass a Government fort without one hundred well-armed men; but once beyond the fort, they would become separated and therein lay the danger.

A captain was appointed by the commander of the fort to take charge. Here we struck the plains proper, or the great American desert, as it was often called, the home of the desperate Indians, degraded half-breeds, and the squaw man—white men with Indian wives—who were at that time either French or Spanish; also the fearless hunters and trappers with nerves of steel, outdoing the bravest Indian in daring and the toughest grizzly in endurance. It is a matter of record that these men of iron were capable and some did amputate their own limbs. A knife sharpened as keen

Fort Carney, Nebraska, 1859

as a razor's edge would cut the flesh; another hacked into a saw would separate the bones and sensitive marrow; while an iron heated to white heat seared up the arteries and the trick was done. There was no anaesthetic in those days.

There were also the cattle and mule thieves who lived in the bluffs, miles from the trail of white men, a tough lot of desperadoes, believing in the adage "Dead men tell no tales."

There were the ranchmen at intervals of twenty, fifty and a hundred miles, who sold to the pilgrims supplies, such as canned goods, playing cards, whiskey of the vilest type, and traded worn-out cattle, doctored to look well for a few days and then give out, thus cheating freighters and pilgrims alike.

These adobe ranches were built of sod cut in lengths of from two to four feet, four inches in thickness and eighteen inches in width and laid grass side down. The side walls were laid either single or double, six feet in height, with the end walls tapering upward. A long pole was then placed from peak to peak and shorter poles from side walls to ridge pole. Four inches of grass covered the poles and the same depth of earth completed the structure making the best fortifications ever devised; no bullet was able to penetrate their sides nor could fire burn them. The poles used for building these adobe ranches were in most cases hauled two hundred miles and in some cases three hundred miles.

Wild Animals of the West

On a graceful slope roamed immense herds of buffalo, bands of elk, thousands of antelope, herds of black-and-white-tail deer and the large gray wolf. Coyotes about the size of a shepherd dog would assemble on the high bluffs or invade the camp and make night hideous by their continuous and almost perfect imitation of a human baby's cry, making sleep impossible. The prairie dog, the fierce rattlesnake, and the beautiful little white burrowing-owl, occupied the same hole in the ground, making a queer family combination. Contrary to the belief of all dwellers and travellers of the plains in that day, Colonel Roosevelt claims it is not a fact that the three mentioned animals occupied the same quarters together, and that the story is a myth.

The little prairie dogs had their villages the same as the Indians. I have frequently seen a prairie dog come out and return into the same hole in the ground. I have also seen a beautiful little white owl silently perched at the side of the same hole and finally enter it, and a few moments later a fierce rattlesnake would crawl into the same hole. Whether it was the snake's permanent abode and it went in for a much needed rest, or whether it was an enemy to the others and the snake went in for a game supper of prairie dog puppies and owl squabs, departing by another route, I am unable to say, as I never took the trouble to investigate one of the holes to confirm the fact. If I had, I would in all probability still be digging. However, in this case, I am inclined to give Colonel Roosevelt the benefit of the doubt for the reason that if nature had not created an enemy to check their increase, the prairie dog would now over-run the country, as they multiply faster than any known animal, and are very destructive to the farm. The Government, through its agents, have destroyed thousands every year in the West by distributing poisoned grain. Last, but not least, of the life of the plains was the pole cat. Conscious of his own ability to protect himself, he would often invade the camps at night, making the life of the sleeper miserable.

Trouble *En Route*

After leaving Fort Carney our troubles began. Many of the drivers were as treacherous as the Indians and would bear watching. One of them in our mess was a former bushwhacker, who bore many scars of his former unsavoury life, one of which was the loss of an eye, which did not make him a very desirable acquaintance, much less a companion. He was of an ugly disposition, very seldom speaking to anyone and very few taking the trouble to speak to him. At times he acted as if he had been taking something stronger than coffee, but as we had not camped near any ranch where the poison could be procured, I came to the conclusion that he was a dope fiend. In some mysterious manner we had lost one of our cups, and at each meal for a week it fell to the lot of this particular bushwhacker to get left. He at last broke his long silence, and in anger with oaths, vowed he would not eat another meal without a cup, and would certainly take one from somebody, if obliged to. As soon as the call for grub was heard the next morning, all rushed simultaneously for a cup, and Mr. Bushwhacker got left again. Without ceremony he proceeded to make good his threat, the second cook being his victim.

For his trouble he received a stinging blow over his good eye, and was sent sprawling in the alkali dust. Not being in the least dismayed, he rushed for another and received a similar salute on the jaw, doubling him up and bringing him to the earth. By this time both messes joined in forming a ring and called for fair play. Mr. Perry tried hard to stop it, but was finally convinced that it was better, policy to let them have it out. How many times the fellow was knocked down, I do not remember, but the last round finished him. We carried him to the shady side of his wagon, covered him with a blanket and resumed our meal. On going into corral, we always took our revolvers off and placed them where they could easily be reached. We had been eating but a short time, when the report of a gun rang out and each man fairly flew for his weapons. Indians seldom made an attack except at early morning, when the oxen were being yoked or when we were going into corral at night. To the surprise of everyone Mr. Bushwhacker had taken another lease of life and with a revolver in each hand was firing at anyone his disturbed brain suggested. He was quick of action, firing and reloading with rapidity, and soon had the entire camp playing hide and seek between, around and under the wagons to keep out of the range of his guns, which we succeeded in doing, for not a man was hit. Finally, two of the drivers succeeded in getting behind him and overpowered him. His brother bushwhackers were in for lynching him on the spot, but wiser council prevailed, and his disposal was left to Mr. Perry who sentenced him to be escorted back three miles from the corral and left to walk the remaining two miles to Fort Carney alone. He covered less than a mile when he was captured by the Indians. I was obliged then to drive his team. A few evenings later my chum and friend were lounging by the side of my wagon smoking, and otherwise passing the time away, when finally the conversation turned to the departed driver who by that time had undoubtedly been disposed of by the Indians— not a very pleasant thought—but we consoled ourselves with the fact that no one was to blame but himself. My chum inquired the contents of my prairie schooner, and I replied that I did not know, but would investigate. Suiting the action to the word I crawled in, struck a match, and found a case labelled Hostetters' Bitters. Its ingredients were one drop of Bitters and the remainder, poor liquor. I soon found a case that had been opened, pulled out a bottle and sampled it. The old story came to me about the Irish saloonkeeper and his bartender. I called my chum and asked him if Murphy was good for a drink, he replied, "Has he got it?" "He has?" "He is then!" and we all were. I thought it would be impossible for the secret to be kept, but it was until we were on the last leg to Denver. The entire load consisted of cases of the Bitters. Fights were of frequent occurrence during the remainder of the trip, Mr. Perry being powerless to prevent them.

Arriving at Central City where the Bitters were consigned, the consignee reported to the freighter that the load just received consisted of one-half Bitters, the remainder Platte river water. Each man had twenty dollars deducted from his pay, and a large number of the drivers, in addition, bore earmarks of its effect.

The country from Fort Carney for four hundred miles up the Platte river valley and back from the high bluffs, that skirted the river on either side, was one vast rolling plain with no vegetation except a coarse luxuriant growth of grass in the valley near the river and beyond the bluffs; in spots that were not bare grew the prickly pear, and a short crisp grass of lightish colour and of two varieties—the bunch and buffalo grasses—which were very nutritious, as the cattle thrived and grew fat on them. There was the clear sky and sun by day, with an occasional sandstorm; the moon (when out) and stars by night, but no rain—a vast thirsty desert. On the small islands of the river a few scattered cottonwood trees were to be seen. Their high branches embraced a huge bunch of something that resembled the nest of an American eagle, but on close inspection was found to be the corpse of a lone Indian a long time dead. This was the mode of burial of some of the tribes in the early days, using fur robes or blankets for a casket. There was nothing to relieve the monotony in this desert land, except desperate Indians, immense herds of animal life, daily coaches—when not held back or captured by the Indians or mountain highwaymen—returning freight trains, and the following points where there were adobe ranches: Dog Town, Plum Creek, Beaver Creek, Godfrey's, Moore's, Brever's at Old

California Crossing and Jack Morrow's at the junction of the north and south Platte, Fort Julesburg, Cotton Wood and the Junction, each one hundred miles apart, and John Corlew's and William Kirby near O'Fallow's Bluffs. It was said of these ranchmen that some were honest and some were not; others were in league with the Indians, and cattle and mule thieves, and, as a rule, a bad lot. They traded supplies to the Indians for furs of every kind. The winter passed in hunting, trapping, drinking, and gambling.

O'FALLOW'S BLUFFS

O'Fallow's Bluffs was a point where the river ran to the very foot of the bluffs making it necessary for all of the trains to cross, then again strike Platte river trail at Alkali Creek, the waters of which were poisonous to man and beast. The trail over the bluffs was of sand, and those heavily ladened, white covered prairie schooners would often sink to the hubs, requiring from fifty to seventy-five yoke of oxen to haul them across, often being compelled to double the leading yoke as far back as the wheelers, then doubling again, would start them on a trot, and with all in line and pulling together, would land the deeply sunken wheels on solid ground. It took one entire day to again reach river trail, which was hard and smooth. O'Fallow's Bluffs was a point feared by freighters and emigrants alike. At this point many a band of pilgrims met destruction at the hands of the fiendish redskins of the plains. Directly upon going into camp at night a party of them would ride up, demand coffee, whiskey, or whatever they wanted, and having received it, would massacre the men and children, reserving the women for a fate a thousand fold worse, as they were very seldom rescued by the tardy government, whose agents were supplying the Indians with guns, ammunition and whiskey to carry on their hellish work unmolested.

When captured, which was seldom, were they hung as they deserved? No, the chief with a few others, who stood high in the councils of the tribe, were taken by stage to Atchison, Kansas, there transferred to luxuriantly equipped sleeping cars of that day, and whirled on to Washington; and, in war paint and feather and with great pomp, were presented to their great white father (the President) as they called him.

ABUSES OF THE INDIAN DEPARTMENT

They were then taken in charge by representatives of the Indian department of the government, that in those days was honeycombed with corruption from foundation to dome; a disgraceful and blood-stained spot in the Nation's history. Day after day and night after night they were shown the sights of that great city. The capitol of a free and growing republic whose people respected the constitution their fathers had drafted, signed and fought for. Day after day and night after night they were courted, dined, toasted and wined until they had become sufficiently mellow to be cajoled into signing another peace treaty, and were then given money and loaded down with presents as an inducement to be good. They were then returned to the agency at the fort, having been taken from there and back by those red-nosed, liquor-bloated Indian department guardians of the United States Government and were freely supplied with whiskey until they were willing to part with their cattle, furs, and beaded goods at extremely low figures, in exchange for provisions, guns, ammunition, and liquor at fabulously high prices. Robbed of their money and presents, and in this condition allowed to return to their village, where when they become sober, they would quickly awaken to a realizing sense of how they had been deceived, swindled and robbed.

What could you expect from those copper-coloured savages of the soil after such treatment? With no regard for the treaty they had signed, they would resume the warpath. Revenge, swift and terrible, was meted out to the innocent pilgrims and freighters who had left home, comforts and friends. Hundreds sacrificed their lives by horrible tortures in their heroic efforts to settle the West, unconscious that they were making history for their country and the nation, great.

With no respect for the United States Government, with no respect for the flag with its cluster of stars and stripes of red, white and blue that fired the heart of every living American soldier to win victory at Valley Forge, which gained our independence, Antietam, and San Juan Hill, saved the nation, reunited the union of states in lasting friendship, lifted the yoke of tyranny from an oppressed people; and, as if with one stroke, swept from the high seas two powerful naval squadrons—the pride of the Spanish nation.

Washington, Lincoln and McKinley were backed by the old glory that electrified every loyal American with patriotism to respond to the call of duty for the love of their country and the "Star Spangled Banner," that at that time fluttered high above the parapet of every government fort as an emblem of protection to all that were struggling on and on over that vast expanse of unbroken and treeless plain; can you wonder then that the unspeakable crimes and mistakes of the government of those days still rankle in the breast of every living man and woman that in any way participated in the settlement of the West? If you do, look on the painting of the terrible annihilation of the gallant Custer and his five companies of the Seventh U. S. Cavalry with the old chief, Sitting Bull, and his band of Sioux Indians on the Big Horn River, June 25, 1876, from which not a man escaped to tell the tale, and you may form some conception of the hardships, suffering, and cruelties inflicted on the early pioneer. It was left for the resourceful Remington to vividly portray life and scenes of those days, perpetuating their memory on canvas and bronze for all time. The name of Frederick Remington should not only go down in history as the greatest living artist of those scenes, but his bust in bronze should be given a place in the Hall of Fame as a tribute to his life and a recognition of his great worth.

Chapter 3

An Attack by the Indians

O'Fallow's Bluffs was the most dismal spot on the entire trail. Its high walls of earth and over-hanging, jagged rocks, with openings to the rolling plain beyond, made it an ideal point for the sneaking, cowardly savages to attack the weary pilgrims and freighters. The very atmosphere seemed to produce a feeling of gloom and approaching disaster. The emigrants had been repeatedly instructed by the commander at Fort Carney to corral with one of the trains. Many of the bullwhackers were desperate men, so that the poor pilgrims were in danger from two sources, and very seldom camped near either corral. Our consort was a day's drive in the rear. That evening the emigrants camped about a half mile in advance of our train. It was at this point, when unyoking our oxen at evening that a large band sneaked over the bluffs for the purpose, as we supposed, of stampeding our cattle. They did not take us unawares, however, for we never turned cattle from corral until the assistant wagon boss surveyed the locality in every direction with a field glass, for the tricky redskin might be over the next sand hill.

Fifty good men could whip five times their number, especially when fortified by those immense white covered prairie schooners in corral formation. On they came in single file, their blood-curdling war whoop enough to weaken the bravest. Closer they came, bedecked in war-paint and feathers, their chief in the lead resembling the devil incarnate with all his aids bent on exterminating as brave a band of freighters as ever crossed the plains. Nearer they came, their ponies on a dead run, the left leg over the back, the right under and interlocking the left, firing from the opposite side of them, ducking their heads, encircling the camp and yelling like demons. Their racket, together with the yelping of their mongrel dogs and the snorting and bellowing of the cattle, made it an unspeakable hell. Every man stood to his gun, and from between the wagons, at the command of the wagon boss, poured forth with lightning rapidity his leaden messengers of death. For about an hour they made it very interesting for us. It was almost impossible to hit one as they kept circling the camp, drawing nearer with each circle made. How many were killed we did not know as they carried them off, but from the number of riderless ponies, a dozen or more must have been dispatched to their happy hunting grounds. During the fight a portion of them bore down on the poor pilgrims' camp, in plain sight, and massacred all, running off their cattle and such of their outfit as they wanted.

Savages in Their Glory

Mothers with babes at their sides and with uplifted, clasped hands, implored the cruel warriors for mercy, but it was like pouring water on the desert sands. Crazed by thirst for blood and the scalps of the whites, they knew no mercy. The hatchet-like tomahawk glittering in the evening twilight, held with a vice-like grip in the hand of

INDIANS ATTACKING CORRAL

a cowardly savage, came down at last with such force as to crush through skull and brain, and all was over. We were powerless to render assistance. The scene was heartrending. The depredations of these savages is too revolting to relate, and after completing their hellish work, they sneaked back as they came, keeping up their sickening yell until distance drowned it entirely. Few days passed that they were not seen as evening approached, and after dark we were able to know that they were in the vicinity, watching their opportunity to surprise us at early morning, by signal arrows of fire shot into the heavens to make known their whereabouts to companions. Could these silent bluffs of sand but unfold the butchery and unspeakable outrages inflicted on innocent men, women and children, could the trail through the valley of the Platte, and even more dangerous trail of the Smoky Hill give up its secrets, it would reveal a dark page in the history of our government, which was directly responsible for a great deal of it; responsible in so far as sending unscrupulous peace commissioners to the different agencies to make treaties of peace with tribes of Indians, and who kept them just long enough to become liberally supplied with provisions, clothing, guns, ammunition and whiskey, then ravish and murder in the most diabolical manner pilgrims and freighters alike. On both trails many a silent monument of stone was all that remained of their cruel depredations. Such was not the uncommon work of the fiends, known to readers of fiction as the noble red men of the plains. More dastardly cowards never existed. Their struggles against destiny have long since been broken, and the offspring of those cruel warriors are being educated by a gracious government.

The monotony of that lonesome and tedious tramp was enlivened only by fights among the men, and an occasional lay-over for a day to set the tires of the many wagons, hav-

MASSACRE OF EMIGRANTS

ing had no rain to keep them tight during the entire trip after leaving Atchison, Kansas.

With many encounters and bearing scars received from warring tribes of Indians, we tramped along in moccasin covered feet, now and again throwing our long lashed whips with such force as to awaken the dead-head ox to life and quicker action.

Day after day the same scenery faced us; yet, it was an experience never to be forgotten. We passed Fort Julesburg and Cottonwood with the loss of but three men, arriving late at night after a forced drive at the junction or division of the two trails leading to Denver. The distance to Denver by the "Cut-off" was seventy-five miles; by the river route one hundred miles; but as water was to be found only at long distances on the former, all cattle trains took the river route.

It was early in November, the nights and mornings were cold and frosty, the air exhilarating. We were up the next morning at the usual time, and as the sun rose in all its splendour and warmth, one hundred miles in the far away distance could be seen with the naked eye, the gigantic range of the Rockies whose lofty snow-capped peaks, sparkling in the morning sun, seemed to soar and pierce the clouds of delicate shades that floated in space about them, attracted, as it were, by a heavenly magnet. It was a sight I had not dreamed of, and one that made an impression on my young mind to last through life.

Denver at Last!

When about ten miles from Denver—so we at least thought, and fearless of danger, my chum and myself obtained permission from Mr. Perry to walk to the city over the rolling ground. We tramped until the sun was well up in the heavens. One would think it but a few miles to those mighty and solemn mountains of rocks, so deceptive was the distance, yet, they were twenty miles beyond the city. At noon we knew we had made ten long miles and were completely tired out. We were on the point of taking a rest when I urged my chum to cross the next knoll, and if the city did not loom up we would halt. We did so and to our surprise and joy were right in the city of Denver, the "Mecca" of nearly all Western freighters and distributing point for the far Western territories. It seemed to have risen beneath our feet. The grand old range of mountains with their sky-soaring pinnacles and scenic background of grandeur, together with the surrounding landscape, made it the sight of one's life. Our sixteen mile walk and previous seventy days' living on a diet of bacon, beans, and dried apples, certainly placed us in condition for a civilized meal.

We were directed to a first-class restaurant, both in price and quality of food. We were about famished, and to satisfy our hunger seemed impossible. We ate and ate, and probably would have been eating yet, had not the waiter presented us with a ticket demanding a five dollar gold piece from each, when we decided we had better call a halt, if we intended to remain in the city over night.

An Old Acquaintance

On walking up the street we stepped into the first hotel we came to, the old "Planters," registered, paid for our supper, lodging and breakfast. When about to leave the hotel, who should walk in but a Genevan by name, Michael C. Pembroke, with his arm in a sling. He had been propelled across the plains by mules, and one of the ugly brutes had broken his right arm with one of his ever active hoofs. I asked Michael why the mule kicked him? He replied, "Charlie, I may look foolish but was not fool enough to go back and ask him." Never approach a Missouri mule from the rear, for there certainly will be trouble if you do. He asked if we had any money.

We replied that we would have when paid off.

He advised us to go direct to the Ben Holiday stage office and buy a ticket for the States as soon as we received our pay, as Colorado was no place for boys.

At his suggestion we started out to do the town, and came very near being done ourselves. Colorado at this time was a territory with a governor appointed by the President. Law, except as executed by a vigilance committee, did not amount to much more than the word. If one wished to depart life in full dress, he could be accommodated by simply calling another a liar or cheat at gambling. If desirous of taking a long rest by being suspended by the neck from a limb of the only tree in Denver at that time, which was on the west side of Cherry Creek, all he had to do was to appropriate to himself an ox, mule, or anything of value, and the vigilance committee would manipulate the rope.

The gambling places, which occupied long halls on the ground floor of tall buildings—nearly always on the business street of the city—kept open until the small hours of morning. There was always a brass band in front, and a string band, or orchestra, in the extreme rear, so if one wished to dance, he could select a partner of most any nationality; dance a set, step up to the bar, pay two bits or twenty-five cents for cigars, drinks or both and expend his balance on any game known to the profession, which games occupied either side of the long room.

We had been in the place less than fifteen minutes when bang went a revolver and on the instant the room was in total darkness. I mechanically ducked under a table. Where my companions were, I knew not; I began to think that Mike's advice was about correct, and before emerging wished more than once I was back in my home. When the

MICHAEL C. PEMBROKE

lights were turned on, I discovered my chum occupying a like berth of safety on the opposite side of the room.

Mike had evidently followed his own advice and taken his departure, for he was nowhere to be found. The band struck up a lively tune; the fiddles, a waltz; dancing began, gold and chips commenced to fly, and, if I had not passed through the ordeal, I never would have known anything had happened. The dead were quickly disposed of, the wounded hurried to physicians, and old timers gave it no further thought, as it was of frequent occurrence, and one soon became hardened. Denver at that time was a hotbed of gambling, with murder and lynch law a secondary pastime. Not being deterred by our experience, we continued our sightseeing, ending up at the only theatre in the city, afterwards called the "Old Languish."

Joining the Cattle Train Again

The following afternoon our train reached town and we joined it during the evening to be ready for an early start for Golden City, the entrance to the mountains leading to Black Hawk and Central City where our freight was consigned. The most hazardous part of our trip was before us, one that to this day makes me shiver when I think of it. The first team entered the canyon at 11 a.m. in a blinding snowstorm. The road for nearly the entire distance was hewn from solid rock out of the side of steep mountains, gradually ascending to a great height, then descending to what seemed a bottomless canyon. We finally arrived at Guy Hill, the most dangerous part of the route. It took us one entire day to reach its pinnacle, where we camped for the night. The road at the top was cut through solid rock at a height of twenty feet, seven feet in width and led to a steep precipice. It then made a sharp turn to the right and, in a serpent shape drive, continued to the canyon below.

At this point it was said to be fifteen hundred feet straight down, and a number of outfits had previously gone over its rocky edge and been hurled to destruction by a slight error of judgment on the part of the driver.

The cold and snow, together with summer clothing, made our suffering indescribable. The following morning I started in the lead of the train with a nine thousand pound boiler, with the rear wheels securely locked, and twenty yoke of oxen to haul it to the edge of the precipice. Then discarding all but the wheelers and leaders, we began the descent. There was not room enough on either side for the driver to walk. He generally rode the off ox, but I took my position on the rear of the wagon tongue and found it decidedly the safest place in case of an accident. By night all wagons were safely in the canyon below. The road for nearly the entire distance presented the same dangers, taking ten days to reach our destination from Denver, the entire trip occupying eighty days.

A Thrilling Coach Ride

On receiving our pay, which was our promised salary less twenty dollars for the Hostetter's Bitters, my chum and myself decided to go direct to Denver, our friend remaining in the Mountain City. We boarded a Concord coach with six snow-white horses to wheel us on a dead run over and around steep mountains and through dismal canyons, first on four wheels, then three, then two and occasionally one, keeping us constantly busy retaining our seats and fearing at every turn that we would be dashed into eternity; and yet, it was one of the most picturesque and thrilling rides one could take. Being tossed from side to side in the roomy coach, now and then grabbing a fellow passenger with desperation, gazing down from lofty peaks to yawning chasms below, hearing the crack of the long-lashed whip urging the noble steeds to faster speed, turning the rough, ragged, serpent-shaped drive, thundering through clouds and mist with lightning rapidity, and always in constant terror of a breakdown or error on the part of the fearless driver, gave one a sensation that would nearly make his hair stand on end. During the descent a slight error on the part of the horses or driver, would have hurled all to a horrible death; but those mountain drivers, strapped to their seats, were monarchs of the Rockies and unerring in every move. From among the snow-covered glaciers sparkling in the morning sun, emitting the many tints of a midday storm-bow and presenting a sight of unsurpassed grandeur, we emerged from the mouth of the last canyon and struck the smooth rolling trail. All the way from Golden we were going, it seemed, on the wings of the wind and were landed in Denver on scheduled time.

CHAPTER 4

Denver in 1865

In that period Denver was appropriately called the "City of the Plains." Situated sixteen miles from the base of the nearest Rocky Mountain peak, and six hundred and fifty miles from Atchison, Kansas, the nearest town to the East; while seven hundred miles to the west loomed up as from the very bowels of the earth, the beautiful city of the Mormons, Salt Lake City, Utah. The nearest forts—two hundred miles distant—were Fort Cottonwood to the northeast, Collins to the north and Halleck to the northwest. Its northern limits extended to the South fork of the Platte River; Cherry Creek running through one-third, dividing it into East and West Denver. Its population numbered about five thousand souls. Here was to be found the illiterate man—but a grade above the coyote—lawbreakers of every kind and from every land, to men of culture and refinement. Here it stood, a typical mining town, a monument to the indomitable energy of man in his efforts to settle that barren and almost endless plain and open to the world the Rocky's unlimited hidden gold. Here were brick structures modern for that day, the brick being made from the soil of the territory; a United States mint, a church, a school house, large warehouses, stores, and the home of the *Rocky Mountain Daily News*, which kept one partially in touch with happenings in the faraway states. Isolated from the outside world, it was an ideal place of refuge for those anxious to escape the outraged law. Knights of the green cloth held full sway. Men in every walk in life gambled. A dead man for breakfast was not an uncommon heading for the menu card, the old tree on the west bank of Cherry Creek furnishing the man. Society was just a little exclusive and to gain admission the pass was, "Where are you from?" and in some cases, "Your name in the East."

Desperadoes made one attempt to lay the city in ashes and certainly would have accomplished their purpose had it not been for the timely action of the Vigilance Committee in hanging the ring-leaders. When the guilt of a suspect for any crime was in doubt, he was presented with a horse or mule and ordered to leave between sun and sun and never return. During my four years of residence in Denver there was but one Indian scare and it made a lasting impression on the tablet of my memory. A church bell pealed forth the warning over the thirsty desert of an Indian attack. Business places were closed, the women and children were rushed to the mint and warehouses for protection, armed men surrounded the city, pickets on horseback were thrown out in every direction. Couriers kept thundering back and forth between picket line and those in command and others were despatched to the different Forts for assistance that never came. A look of determination stood out on the face of every one and not a man, from clergyman to desperado, within the confines of the city who would not willingly have given up his life's blood to protect the honour of the women and lives of the little ones. For three weary days and the same number of nights the terrible suspense lasted, but no Indian came. It was a false alarm.

Denver, in its early settlement, was never attacked by the Indians except in isolated cases. The only reason that I ever heard given for their not doing so was that they knew not their strength, for there was no time in the sixties that they could not have swooped down on the place, massacred all and buried the little mining town in ashes.

Secured Work Again

For a young man to obtain work other than oxen or mule driving, we were told, was simply impossible. Not being deterred, however, by this discouraging information we at once started out to secure work. Board was twenty-five dollars a week in gold, and you had to furnish your own sleeping quarters, so not to secure work at once would quickly reduce our wealth. We had called on nearly all of the business places, when my chum secured a position with a grocer and freighter. As for myself, I received little encouragement but finally called at a large restaurant where I was offered work. I told the proprietor it was a little out of my line, but he told me that if I could not find a position to suit me, I should walk in at any time, pull off my coat and go to work, which I did three days later. About the tenth day the proprietor told me his lease expired and that the man who owned the building was going to conduct the business. He came in that afternoon, and I was introduced to him. Before leaving he stepped into the office and informed me that he wanted a man next to him; or, in other words, an assistant and that the former proprietor had given me a good recommend and he thought that I would suit him. He made me a tempting offer and I accepted. The restaurant was located on Blake street, one of the then principal business streets of the city, and kept open until early morning as did the gambling places in the immediate vicinity. I soon discovered that the new proprietor could neither read or write and that he conducted one of the largest private club rooms in the city where gambling was carried on without limit. He paid me a large salary and allowed me everything my wild nature craved. I had charge of the entire business as well as his bank account.

The restaurant was the headquarters of nearly all oxen and mule drivers and also of the miners who came from the mountains in winter, and were of the toughest type of men of that day. All professional oxen and mule drivers after making one round trip to the river and points in the far Western territories were paid off in Denver and many of them would deposit with me, for safe keeping, a large share of their dangerously and hard earned dollars. They would then start out to do the town, now and then taking a chance at one of the many gambling games, always returning for more money, which I would give them; and this they would continue until all was expended except enough to keep them a week, when sober, and a commission for doing the business, for which I was careful to look out. An individual who bore the name of "One Eye Jack" boarded with us and I could always depend upon him in time of trouble. His vocation for a long time was a mystery, until one evening, as I was passing down a side street, he popped out from an alley and with uplifted blackjack would have felled and robbed me had he not recognized the unearthly yell I gave. I forgave him, and afterwards he doubled his energies to protect me and on more than one occasion saved my life. When in his professional clothes he was a tough looking customer and could fight like a bull dog. He was always liberally supplied with someone else's money. Yet with all his bad traits, his word was as good as his gold; but like other similar individuals that infested Denver at that time, he finally went to the end of his tether, and was presented by the Vigilance Committee with a hemp collar that deprived him of his life.

Before his demise, however, a party of ten tough-looking individuals entered the restaurant and, in forceful language, demanded the best the country offered in eatables and drink. My friend, or would-be-murderer, was in at the time and I noticed a look of cunning pleasure steal over his rough countenance. The strangers were dressed in corduroy trousers, velveteen coats, slouch hats and black ties. Their shirts and collars of red flannel made a conspicuous appearance and caused their undoing later. After seeing them well cared for, I returned to the office and calling Jack inquired his opinion of the gents.

"Well," he replied, "I may be mistaken but I will just bet you a ten spot they are road agents." "Yes," I said, "I am inclined to agree with you, but keep mum."

You may think it strange I did not give this bold highwayman away; but life in those days was sweet and I had no desire to have that young life taken so I followed Comanche Bill's advice and strictly minded my own business. If I had not, I would not be living today.

Highwaymen of the West

Two mornings later on entering for breakfast one of the band had his head done up in a bandage. From words he dropped I was satisfied that Jack or one of his cronies had been improving their spare time by relieving him of his over abundance of gold. The reckless manner in which they disposed of their money and their conversation when flushed with wine betrayed their true characters and stamped them a murderous band of mountain highwaymen who had made their headquarters in the fastnesses of the Rockies, near the overland mountain trail and there devoted their time to holding up stage coaches, compelling the driver with a shot from a carbine to halt, descend, disarm and be quiet. The passengers were then ordered to alight and stand in a row, continually being covered with guns by a part of the band and by others relieved of their personal effects. Then the stage coach was systematically gone through together with the Wells Fargo & Co's. safe, which often contained gold into the thousands. These hold-ups were not infrequent and were the fear of all who were obliged to pass through these canyons of robbery and often death. The bunch that we harboured were undoubtedly as bold a band of robbers and murderers as ever infested the silent caves of the Rockies. Could their dingy walls but talk they would reveal crimes unspeakable. I knew there were many strangers in town and was almost certain their every movement was watched; nor was I mistaken. The seventh day after their arrival a young school teacher whom I knew by sight called at the restaurant and inquired by name for one of the band. I asked if he knew him. He replied, no more than that he had met him in one of the corrals of the city and had been offered free passage to the States if he would do their cooking. I told him of my suspicions and all I knew about them and advised him not to go with them, but like many others he gave no heed. Two days later they were missed at meal time. The next morning word came by courier that the entire band including the school teacher were dangling by the neck from the branches of cottonwood trees twelve miles down the Platte River with their pockets inside-out and outfits gone. Thus was meted out to innocent and guilty alike the Vigilance Committee justice, which was not of uncommon occurrence.

Mr. Pembroke secured a position at Black Hawk, Colorado, in the year 1865, with the first smelter works erected

ROAD AGENTS HOLDING UP STAGE COACH

in the Rocky Mountains. He was employed in the separating department where sulphur was freely used, and he inhaled much of the fumes emitted therefrom, which was the direct cause of a severe illness.

He fought retirement for a long time, but was finally forced to give up.

The latter part of February, 1886, he arrived in Denver on his way to his home in Geneva, N.Y., but remained with me at the restaurant for ten days where he was cared for and given the best of medical aid available in those days.

He finally prevailed on a mule freighter to take him as a passenger to Atchison, Kansas. Arriving at Fort Carney, Nebraska, he had a relapse and was ordered by the commander of the fort to be placed in the army hospital for treatment, where he remained until able to continue his journey by stage to Atchison, thence by rail home.

He left Colorado with the full determination of returning on recovering his health. A mother's influence, however, changed his plans and he finally decided to remain in the East. He purchased a grocery business and conducted it with great success until his death, March 17th, 1910. By his strict attention to business, square dealing, genial disposition and original wit, he gained the confidence and respect of his fellow-men. He was buried in St. Patrick's cemetery in his home city where a surviving sister has caused to be erected an appropriate and costly monument to his memory.

NEW EMPLOYMENT

I remained with the restaurant keeper one year, when through the assistance of influential men that boarded at the restaurant, I secured a position with a grocer. Shortly after entering his employ I made the acquaintance of an ex-army officer, a graduate of West Point and a well edu-

VIGILANCE COMMITTEE JUSTICE

cated man, who afterwards became my boon companion. At that time he was an ex-pork merchant from Cincinnati; an eccentric old fellow without chick or child, and with plenty of money to loan at 3% a month. He owned a large warehouse on Cherry Creek in West Denver where he slept and did his own cooking. His evenings were passed at the store and many were the nights that we told stories and otherwise enjoyed ourselves. He was a silent member of the firm and I was wise enough to keep on the right side of him. During that time the head of the firm ran for Congress on the Democratic ticket. Such an election I never want to see or go through again. Large wagons loaded with barrels of all kinds of liquor on tap were driven from poll to poll. Many more ballots were cast in each precinct than there were voters and by night nearly the entire male portion of the inhabitants were a drunken, howling mass. The outcome of the election resulted in the governor giving the Democratic nominee the certificate of election; the Secretary of the territory favouring the Republicans. The governor left the city that night and never returned. The contest terminated in a Republican Congress seating the Republican candidate, and Andrew Johnson—then President of the United States—appointing the Democratic candidate governor of Colorado. A year from that time General Grant was inaugurated, and shortly afterwards the governor's head went into the basket and mine fell on the outside.

On another occasion there was to be a prize fight at Golden City, sixteen miles from Denver. My friend, the ex-pork merchant, I could see was anxious to attend but did not wish to lower his standard of dignity by doing so, so the subject was not mentioned save in a casual way until the morning of the fight, when he entered the store, puffing and blowing, stamping the floor with his hickory cane and mopping his crimson brow with an old-fashioned bandana handkerchief, said "Charley, let's go to that infernal fight. I don't approve of it, but let's go."

"All right," I said. I was in for any kind of sport.

An Experience in Mule Riding

I left everything, locked the store and started out to procure a rig, but found there were none to be had for love or money. The only article of propulsion we could hire were saddle mules. Both quickly mounted and on a slow trot started for the ring. We had been there less than an hour when both of us became thoroughly disgusted and started on the return trip. When about seven miles from Denver and going at a lively pace—for a mule—the Major's animal stiffened both front legs, and placing his hoofs firmly in the sandy road, permitted the Major's chunky little body to pass over his head and through space for about ten feet, landing, with much force, on his stomach. The old fellow was an artist at curse words and the more I laughed the more he cursed. He was a sprightly little fellow and on gaining his feet grabbed for the bridle, but Mr. Mule shook his head, made a side step, and the devil could not have caught him again until he reached the barn. I dismounted and with much difficulty my friend scrambled into my saddle, with myself on behind. But my long-eared critter objected and the fun commenced. He bunted and kicked. All of a sudden his hind quarters rose and like lightning his long lanky legs shot high into the air. First, I went off, and on gaining a sitting position with mouth, ears and eyes full of sand, I witnessed a spectacle befitting the clumsiest bareback rider on one of their first lessons. The old Major had both arms affectionately entwined around the mule's thick neck and was hanging on with desperation. Up and down went the hind quarters of that unkind brute, bunting and kicking, the Major's little body keeping taps with the ups and downs and every time he caught his breath he let out a war whoop that would do credit to a Comanche brave. The old mule finally dumped him all in a heap and followed his mate to Denver. Such an appearance as both presented, each blaming the other for our misfortune and vowing we would never be caught at another prize fight. Lame, bruised, and crestfallen, we walked the remainder of the way into Denver. Each cautioned the other to say nothing of our misfortune; but the two Mauds had carried the news ahead, and we were the laughing stock of the town for the next nine days.

At another time I was attending a performance in the "Old Languish Theatre," when from the stage I was informed I was wanted in the bar room of the building, a necessary adjunct to all western theatres in those days. Upon entering I was taken by the hand by one of those trusty and warm-hearted stage drivers of the plains and Rockies, and told that my chum had been caught in one of those treacherous mountain snow storms on the Catchla Purder River two miles above La Port and was badly frozen, and, if he didn't receive medical aid at once, could not survive. I left the theatre at once and commenced preparing plans for the trip. I started unaccompanied the following afternoon at 2:30 o'clock on a one hundred fifty mile ride.

A Ride in a Storm

My conveyance was a long old-fashioned buggy. The buggy, which was well filled with straw, blankets, medicine, grub, and a commissary bottle, had two good roadsters hitched in front to wheel me to the rescue of my friend or to an ignominious death. I had not only Indians to fear, but the treacherous elements. The trail ran close along the base of the mountains. It was a lovely May day. I was obliged

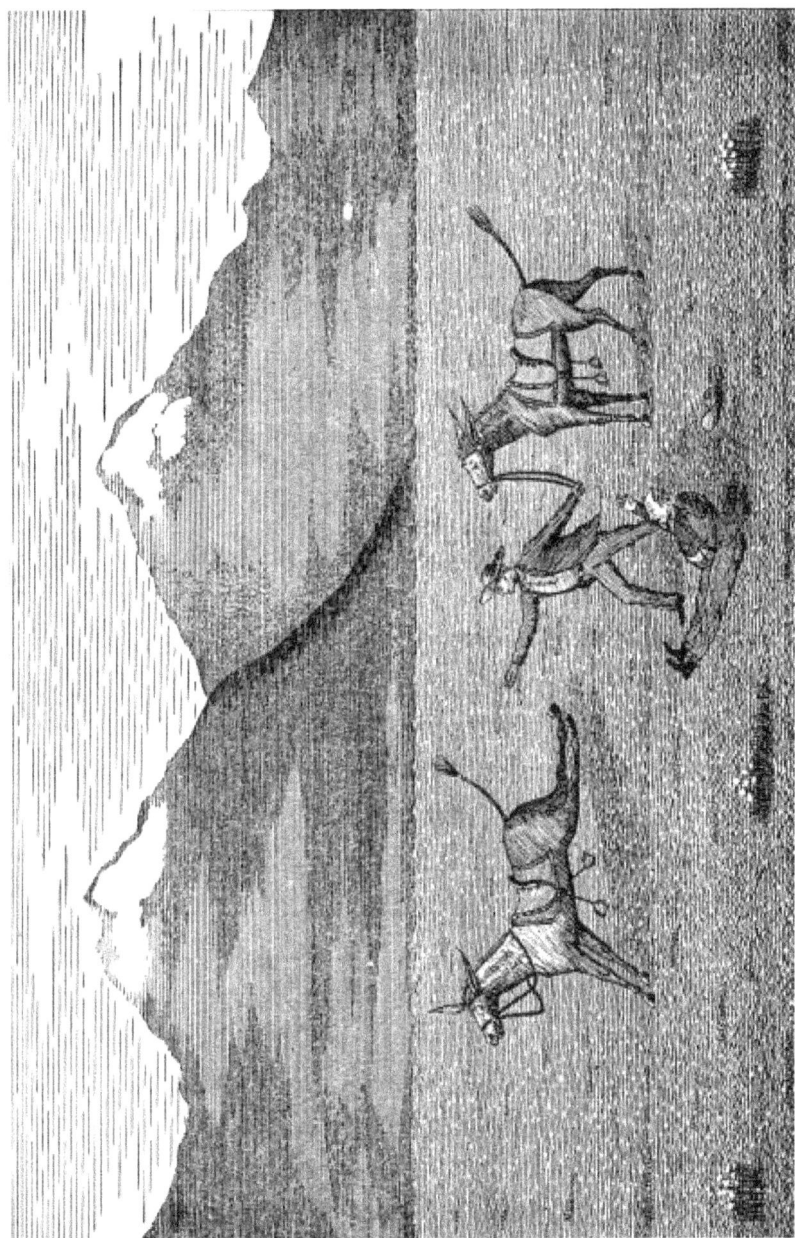

Returning from prize fight

to make thirty-two miles that night to reach cover. Less than half of the distance had been travelled when the wind veered suddenly to the north, mild at first, then a hurricane of anger, roaring and blowing with such force as to nearly upset the buggy. Dark clouds gathered and floated around those silent peaks of ages. Lightning darted hither and thither among the stalwart pines, which were creaking, bending and crashing. Clap after clap of thunder pealed through and from those dismal canyons, vibrating between Nature's slopes of granite, quartz and rock. The din was fearful, rain fell at first, then turned to snow. Just before it became dark I adjusted the front piece of the buggy. My compass was useless. I urged my faithful steeds to faster speed, and at the same time gave them the rein. As I did so, they left the trail. Cold and chilled to the marrow or very bone, I took frequent drafts from the commissary bottle, and fought with all my power against sleep, but it was useless.

On gaining partial consciousness two squaws were bending over me rubbing me with all their Indian strength and a third forcing something warm down my throat. Men, rough of dress, were smoking and playing cards. Revolvers, chips and gold was in front of each, with plenty of the latter in the centre of the table. I knew not if they were friends or mountain highwaymen. Many claim that horses are dumb brutes with no instinct, but that faithful pair on leaving the trail avoided a long bend and made straight for the adobe stage ranch, sixteen miles away. On reaching it, they ran the buggy-pole through the only opening of that mud shack rousing the inmates to action and bringing me to safety.

The large Concord coach filled with passengers soon arrived from Denver, and owing to the severity of the storm, put up for the night. The time was passed in smoking, drinking and playing cards. At six o'clock the next morning the coach pulled up at the door. The storm was over, but not the wind. The cold was intense. My team soon came up, but their ears and noses were badly frost bitten and otherwise showed the effects of the storm. I followed the coach but for a short distance only, as the snow which was drifting badly obliterated the trail. The six black horses on the coach were too much for my two bays and soon left me far in the rear. My compass had been lost and by noon I was back at the ranch I had previously left, the horses having made nearly a complete circle without my knowledge. I secured another compass and at nine o'clock that evening rolled into La Port, a city of adobe ranches, and stage station, where I put up for the night. (A place of two or three houses in those days was called a city.) I was informed that my chum was two miles up the river and in bad shape. The next morning I was up at day break. After grub I started and found my companion quartered in a little old log cabin at the base of the mountains, and being cared for by an aged squaw and her daughter—the old buck being out caring for the cattle. My chum had encountered the same kind of a storm as his rescuer, and unable to find his way was obliged to remain out the entire night and only one hundred feet from the cabin. Both of his feet were badly frozen. The Indians had done everything possible for him. The daughter, for an Indian, was extremely pretty, and I soon discovered that she was very much taken with my chum. I applied the remedies which I had brought. Then the little Indian maiden bundled him up, and with the promise that he would return they parted.

We were at once off on the return trip and arrived at the stage ranch, where I was cared for the previous night at just six o'clock. On driving up to the door of the station all three of the reaches of the buggy broke and gently dropped us to the ground. Fortunately there was a blacksmith connected with the station and I assisted him through the long night, forging reaches and repairing the buggy. At daylight we were off, reaching Denver in safety at 3:30 that afternoon and making the trip in just three days.

Both of my chum's feet had to be amputated at the insteps. He was very grateful and quite conscious of the fact that true friendship still existed.

Before leaving the governor's employ, I accompanied a mule train of ten wagons with supplies for the Ute tribe of Indians who lived in one of the parks of the mountains in the vicinity of Pike's Peak. The Utes, at that particular time, were on friendly terms with the white men as there was a treaty of peace existing between them and the Government.

Chapter 5

A Proof of Marksmanship

We took with us a Mr. Baker, who was conceded to be one of the best guides, hunters, trappers and interpreters of that day, with a heart as large as an American bison, and as tender as a child's. But when his anger was aroused by danger or treachery, the very devil seemed to possess him; he had the courage of a lion, and was a dead shot. We had been friends for a long time, and on more than one occasion he had proved a true one.

The park was an ideal summer resort, an extended plateau with acres of fresh green grass, wild flowers, and virgin soil. In the centre was a beautiful lake, its ice cold water well stocked with the finny tribe of speckled mountain trout, the delight of the angler. The park was enclosed by mountains of great height and grandeur, their rocky slopes were dotted with spruce, pine, and cottonwood, and capped with ages of crystal snow, presenting a sight more pleasing to the eye than the Falls of Niagara, and a perfect haven for an Indian maiden's love dream.

We had been in camp but a few days when Mr. Baker

informed me that the young bucks, as the men of the tribe were called, wanted us to join in shooting at a target. After Mr. Baker and myself had made a few bull's eyes, they proposed we two should choose sides, and we did so. The teams were very evenly matched, making the game interesting. In the meantime, I had been presented to the chief in true Indian fashion and in turn was made known by him to his squaw, young bucks and maidens. The Indians had their tribal laws and customs as well as the white man and were required to live up to them. The maidens were two in number, their ages fourteen and seventeen moons respectively; the latter a picture of Indian beauty, perfect in every feature, form and carriage, a rare model for an artist. They were nearly always found together. At first they were quite reserved, but finally we became fast friends; we would ramble, hunt, fish from canoes and sail the placid waters of the little lake.

Early on the morning of the tenth day Mr. Baker entered my tent with a troubled look. I bade him good-morning and inquired the cause. Without fencing, he asked me if I wanted to be a squaw man. I asked him what the devil he was getting at.

An Offer of Matrimony

He replied, "All there is to it, the old chief has taken a great liking to you, and wants you to marry Weenouah, his oldest daughter. He has plenty of money, and his horses and cattle run into four figures."

"That is no inducement," I said, "and it could never be."

Mr. Baker asked, "How are you going to get out of it?"

I replied, "I have been in lots of tight places, as you know, and have always managed to squeeze through, and I'll get out of this one in some way."

Little did either of us dream at that time of the manner,

or rather the sacrifice, that one of us was doomed to bear, for me to escape the wrath of the old chief, when informed I would not marry his daughter. Fate decreed he was never to be so informed, but instead, a most cruel and unfortunate accident was to provide the means.

That afternoon the young bucks were again anxious to test their skill at the target. We all used the same carbine, which contained seven cartridges, one in the gun barrel and six in a magazine in the butt of the gun. Mr. Baker and I always tossed up a pebble to see who had first shot. As Mr. Baker won the first chance, he took aim and pulled the trigger and such an explosion as took place will never be forgotten. Everyone was stunned by its force. When the smoke had cleared, poor Baker's body was found lying on the ground with the lower jaw torn from its place. On recovering from the shock the young bucks fairly flew for the Indian medicine man. I quickly reached the corral and informed the wagon boss of the accident. He at once ordered the mules brought up. The light wagon was supplied with straw, blankets, commissary bottle and grub. Six of the fastest mules were hitched to the wagon and selecting two of the mulewhackers gave instruction for his care en route. I took the lines and quickly drove to the spot where poor Baker had fallen. Just as soon as the flow of blood had been checked and his wounds dressed we raised him gently and placed him in the wagon. Without a word I mounted the driver's box and drove for all there was in those six mules, reaching Denver late the following night. Some who read this narrative may be sceptical, but it is a fact, nevertheless, that poor Baker recovered for I saw him a year later, but he could partake of liquid food only. The once stalwart form of that brave man, now emaciated and wasted to a mere skeleton, still stood erect.

My whole heart went out to him who, in years past, had hunted the antelope, deer, elk and buffalo; fought the cowardly savages and desperadoes on the thirsty plains and amidst the ragged slopes of the Rocky Mountains; penetrated the silent recesses of the dismal canyons and caves; crossed the snow covered divides; faced danger of every conceivable nature; and at last, although maimed for life, was grateful that he had escaped death and thankful in the thought that he had done his share in the settlement of the then Far West. As I gazed into his once keen eyes and beheld that shrivelled face, my heart wrung with remorse, for I knew he had keenly suffered. Tears filled my eyes and trickled down my weather-beaten and sun-tanned boyish face, and I knew he accepted it as an emblem of my sorrow for being the innocent cause, in a measure, of his cruel misfortune. Thus, by the flip of a pebble was my life spared, but at the expense of a true friend.

CHAPTER 6

On to Leavenworth

The next summer I was not very well, and so I made a trip to Leavenworth, Kansas, by the Southern or Smoky Hill route. We made the trip by mule train of twenty wagons with six mules hitched to each. The driver rode the nigh mule and with one line guided the team. If he wanted the leaders to go to the right he simply jerked fast or slow, depending on how quick he wanted to make the turn; if to the left, a steady or quick pull. The Indians on this trail were more numerous than on the Platte and scarcely a day passed that they were not to be seen, and continually trying to drive off our stock.

We did not receive any great scare until we reached the Big Blue River where on the fourth day of July at ten o'clock in the morning a large Concord coach filled with passengers and a small guard of the United States soldiers, which had previously passed us, were awaiting our arrival before daring to proceed. On reaching the crest of the bluff leading to the valley of the river we saw hundreds of Sioux Indians, in war paint and feathers, camped on the opposite side in the underbrush and woods, and in the main trail directly in our path.

We at once went into corral. Thirty men against a horde of savages, if they were there to dispute our right of progress, was not a pleasant position to be placed in nor a fitting manner in which to celebrate the glorious Fourth. Consultations were numerous and all took part. The redskins, camped in plain sight, were hurrying to and fro, evidently in council like ourselves. To the right of the trail was a dense wood close to the river bank; on the left was a high perpendicular bluff, its sides unscalable, so our route was a genuine death trap, should they attack us. After grub all gathered in a circle and with pipes we proceeded with our last council. The situation was talked over from every point as to what the Indians might do or might not do. We finally arrived to the conclusion that they had the best of us whatever move we made. A majority vote decided to proceed with every man for himself in case of attack. Our wagons were empty which was a little in our favour as we could go on a mule trot or gallop. The coach filled with passengers was placed in the lead; and, being the youngest of the party, they were considerate enough to let me follow, and I did so as closely as possible. On reaching the river bottom, the driver of the coach started his horses on a run and the lash was put to every mule. We were all yelling like demons and on our approach the Indians left the trail and took to the river, thinking that we were a hundred or more strong. All passed safely through that valley of what might have been a horrible massacre. The unearthly racket we made was undoubtedly our salvation, but we were not out of danger by any means and continued our flight until eleven p.m. when we went into corral for food and rest. At three a.m. we again struck the trail and it is well that we did, for those blood-thirsty redskins laid death and destruction in their wake and came very near overtaking us a day later. Arriving at Leavenworth, I boarded a Missouri River palace for St. Louis, thence to New Orleans.

A False Friend

On returning to St. Louis, I met a Westerner that I knew only by sight, and by him was induced to remain over a few days and take in the city. I did and was scooped. On the third morning I went through my pockets and the bed, piece by piece, dumping its contents in the centre of the room, but my roll was gone. At once I sought my friend, but he was nowhere to be found. Plain case of misplaced confidence. He had made a touch. In my desperation, I made a confident of the caretaker of the hotel register. Being of a sympathetic nature, he consoled me with an invitation to stimulate, which I did. Being without a trunk, I was informed on my arrival it was customary to pay as you enter; fortunately I had a meal to my credit. I was in good condition, having had sufficient victuals to last the day, after which I proceeded to the river front and here discovered a boat bound for Omaha. I boarded her, sought out the steward, and applied for a position. He replied that he did not want any help.

"Well, I suppose you will let a fellow work his way, won't you?"

His answer was "Get off this craft," and without further talk, in not a very gentlemanly manner he assisted me.

On landing, I was mad clear through, and made up my mind I was going on that boat, and I did go. Just before the gang plank was pulled in I walked on board, keeping a sharp lookout for the steward. After I had avoided him for an hour and just as I was on the point of congratulating myself, I bumped into him.

"You on board?"

"It looks very much as if I were in evidence."

He grabbed me by the coat collar and hustled me before the captain. I told a straight story, and he, being a man, told the steward to take me up to the kitchen and set me to work. He did, and had his revenge in seeing that it was nearly continuous. After supper I worked the dish racket until twelve o'clock. At three the next morning he awoke me out of a sound sleep and set me to cleaning the woodwork of the cabin. Another of my desirable duties was to wash and polish the silver, throwing the water over the sides of the boat.

AN ALERT STEWARD

After dinner of the second day I proceeded with the tin bucket to the side of the boat and overboard went its contents, including three silver spoons. The spoons had no sooner left the bucket than I felt something of great force come in contact with the seat of my trousers. For a moment I thought surely perpetual motion had been discovered. Turning I was face to face with that infernal steward. Nor did that end my troubles for during the entire trip that particular locality of my person was the target for that fellow's boot. With a terrible oath, he informed me that my landing would be reached about midnight a day later and was called Wood Pile Landing. A short time before reaching the place, I was hustled from my bunk by the steward and in no gentle manner forced to the bow of the boat. The night was pitch dark, and produced a decidedly lonesome feeling in the one that was to be put off at a wood pile on the edge of an immense forest and undoubtedly miles from a dwelling. As the boat reached the bank, not even waiting for the gang plank to be shoved out, the old sinner gave me a push and at the same time applied the now familiar boot. I reached the earth on all fours. My first thought was to present him with a rock, but I curbed my temper, for I had no idea of deserting the old ship.

In those days the boilers of the boats were fired with cord wood purchased of the planters and delivered on the bank of the river. All boats plying on the Missouri River at that time were flat bottom with paddle wheel at the stern. Two long heavy poles were carried at the bow and worked with a windlass, being used to raise the bow of the boat when becoming fast on a sand bar. The pilot was obliged to keep a continuous lookout for these bars, as the channel was treacherous and changed often.

On approaching the river bank one of the deck hands would jump off with the bow line and make fast to a stump or tree, then the stern line was thrown to him and similarly connected. Then the negro deck hands would proceed to carry on the wood on their bare shoulders to the tune of a Southern plantation melody. When ready to start the bow line was cast off, the paddle wheel was started by the engine, and by means of the steering gear the craft was swung out into the stream, then the stern line was thrown aship, and the boat was off—but not without the steward's victim. No sooner had the coloured gentlemen reached the deck, than I followed. Waiting until all was quiet aboard, I sought my berth. The next morning I proceeded with my work as if nothing had happened. I anticipated the steward's next move would be to throw me overboard, and in that belief told the cook of what he had done the previous night. At that point he came in, and on discovering me said, "You here again," his face purple with rage. His right foot at once became restless, he made a rush for me, but the cook with butcher-knife in hand prevented the action of said foot, and my troubles with that gentleman were over.

We soon reached Leavenworth, and I left the boat without regret, but a much wiser youth. I went to the First National Bank of Leavenworth, drew my money, and after a few days' rest, I again embarked for Denver astride a mule. We saw plenty of Indians, but as the train was a long one they did not molest us.

On reaching the city of the plains I at once hunted up my old friend, the Major, who introduced me to the head of a firm of contractors, who were at that time engaged in getting out ties in the "Black Hills," for a portion of the Union Pacific railroad, then under construction. He told me that he wanted a man to go there and straighten out a set of books that a former employee had left badly mixed. He also took the trouble to inform me that the country was alive with Indians, and that the man who went there took big chances; and, if I were at all timid, I had better not accept the position. My friend gave me a strong recommend and I clinched the matter by telling the gentleman that I was not afraid of man, ghost or Indian. He replied that I was just the man he was in search of, and would give me five hundred dollars in gold, a good horse and pay all expenses; that I should get my traps and be at the Planter's Hotel for dinner.

He expected his two partners from the east to inspect the camp and business, and everything was to be in readiness to depart on their arrival. Our conveyance was a full sized Concord coach with six good mules to draw it. The boot of the coach contained the best of everything to eat and drink—the latter being just as essential in that country as gun and ammunition. The partners were detained en route, and did not arrive until the second day, when they wished to rest and see the western sights, so we did not leave until the fourth day. Two Denverites accompanied us, making six in the party.

The first afternoon we made thirty-two miles, and camped near a stage station, where they keep, for the weary pilgrims, supplies and the rankest kind of corn juice known to the professional drinker.

The following morning we made an early start, and before noon rolled into La Port, on the Cachella Pondre River, the only settlement on the trail to the hills. We put up at the stage station for the night. There we met a drover, and a party of cow boys with one thousand head of California broncos bound for the States. Those cowboys were as wild as western life could make them, yet, a jolly good lot.

During the evening, at the suggestion of someone, a poker game was started which lasted all night, and in the morning those who had indulged in the game were not feeling any too good—especially the losers—but, nevertheless, they all strolled over to the large adobe corral to see our party off. Mr. A——, the head of the firm of contractors, had his large winnings safely concealed in a chamois bag placed close to his hide, where all wise men of the West carried their money in those days.

The drover had been a heavy but good loser. When about ready to hitch up our mules he called out to Mr. A——, "I'll go you six of my best broncos against five hundred dollars that you haven't a man in your outfit that can drive the d——d brutes a mile and return."

The contractor approached me and asked if I thought I could do it. I told him that I was willing to take the chance.

Without another word he walked over to where the drover was standing and informed him that he would take the bet, provided he would have his cowpunchers hitch the little devils to the coach.

"Agreed," shouted the old fellow in no uncertain language.

The boys turned to the work with a will; for the fun expected, even if I received a broken neck for my daredevil recklessness, excited them to the highest pitch.

The reader has undoubtedly seen in the Wild West circuses the old-fashioned overland coach hung by heavy springs from front to rear axle. One of the most uncomfortable conveyances to ride in ever invented, especially for the driver, for, if the coach was not heavily loaded, when the front wheels dropped into a hole the old ramshackle thing was liable to topple over on the animals; and, if the driver was not securely strapped to the seat when the rear wheels reached the hole, he would land some distance in the rear. The contractor had the old ark properly balanced before starting, so I had no excuse to worry from that source.

The cowpunchers selected one bronco each and after a half hour's hauling, pulling and coaxing succeeded in hitching them to the coach. I climbed to the seat and was securely strapped with a large leather apron. Then I gathered up the lines and placed myself solidly for the start.

The whip socket contained a hickory stick five feet long with a lash twelve feet in length attached to one end. I gave the word to let them go, but the little broncos thought different and balked. The number of times they bucked and threw themselves, started and bucked again, would be impossible to say. Finally the contractor accused the drover of being in collusion with his cowpuncher in order to win the wager by holding the broncos back and a volley of words of not very mild character ensued, after which the six cowboys, three on either side of the team, stood off six feet. The noise made by the cracking of their whips their everlasting yelping made the excitement stronger than before, and I was off on the wildest ride I ever took. A hurdle jumper would not stand much of a chance with one of those wild broncos.

It was a lovely June morning and the bracing air of Colorado made me feel as wild as the young animals that were fast wheeling me over the dangerous trail and possibly into a camp of hostile Indians. I gave no thought to danger for I was too busy keeping the fiery little beasts to the trail. They were going at breakneck speed with no sign of tiring, so I let them go enjoying the sport even more than they. My hat went flying with the wind, I looked back, but could not see the ranch. How far I had left it behind, or what distance I had covered, I knew not.

At last I came to myself and realized for the first time what terrible danger I was in. Slowly turning the team to the right, I began a circle, hardly perceptible at first, but finally again reaching the trail. On the return trip, I plied the long lash to the leading pair. They shot forward faster than ever, all steaming with foam and covered with lather. At a great distance to the south I could see a party of Indians riding in the same direction. This additional danger seemed fairly to intoxicate me and I plied the whip with all my strength. The corral loomed up and then the stage station. The others, with hands in their pockets and mouth agap, were holding their breath; and, as we wheeled past them, the cowboys lashing the broncos, a mighty shout went up. I had won the wager and was the lion of the day.

We did not make a start until the following morning. We fastened the broncos together and tied the leader to the rear of the coach, and thus resumed our journey to the hills, where we safely arrived two days later, but minus four of the treacherous brutes. At night we always picketed them with the mules and the four that were lost had pulled their picket irons and undoubtedly gone to join the much read of "wild horses of the plains."

The camp in the hills consisted of shanties for fifteen

hundred men, saw mill, and outfit store. The latter included in its stock plenty of the best kind of liquor. Each man was allowed three drinks a day and no more.

I had the books straightened out in due time and one day the contractor discovered he would soon be out of flour, and the nearest point at which it could be purchased was La Port, seventy-five miles distant. The Indians were troublesome, and each man who was asked refused to go, with one exception. The contractor finally made me a tempting offer to accompany a driver of a six mule team. I accepted, and at break of day the next morning we started. My companion on that dangerous trip was a plucky son of the Emerald Isle. We camped that night on Lodge Pole Creek. On the opposite side was an adobe ranch, and an immense stockade owned by a Frenchman with a Sioux squaw for a wife.

In our hurried start we had forgotten our tobacco, and without it my companion seemed lost. After grub I mounted my horse, and crossed over the creek to procure some. On making my wants known, I was freely supplied with tobacco, and was also informed that before we arrived they had been fighting the Indians for some time; that one of the cowboys had an arm badly shattered; and that they feared another attack the next morning. I returned to camp and told my companion of our danger.

A Welcome Haven

After giving the animals plenty of feed and rest, we again took the trail at 4:30 a.m. As the day dawned, with the aid of a field glass, I discovered Indians swooping down on the ranch with the stockade at breakneck speed, and others coming in our direction. I told Patrick to urge the mules to a gallop. He suspected the cause and did so at once. Over the rolling ground we flew until the sun was well up in the heavens, and as each hour passed the redskins gained on us, until at last they could be seen with the naked eye. The harsh and cruel war-whoop of those blood-thirsty savages echoed and re-echoed back from the distant hills, and over the desolate plains until men and beasts were crazed to desperation. The lash was put to the already tired mules, and we strained every nerve to reach the crest of the next knoll, hoping against hope for succour. On they came, their war whoops for scalps and the white man's blood was now continuous. The long feared report of their rifles was at last heard; bullets pierced our canvas covered wagon. We made a last desperate effort and reached the summit of the bluff. Not a half a mile from its base was a large corral of white covered wagons. Down the incline we flew, looking neither to the right nor the left, and, on reaching the corral, both men and beasts fell into a heap exhausted.

The red devils rode to the top of the hill, and the war whoop of anger they sent up rings in my ears at times to this very day.

That evening we again took the trail and made the remainder of the trip by night drives. Reaching La Port the third morning, we secured our load and after giving the animals a much needed rest we started on the return trip. The fourth morning we arrived at the ranch with the stockade. Three mornings after we reached the foot of the hills where the company had a log cabin for their hunters and trappers, who, with their trusty rifles, furnished antelope, deer and buffalo meat for their small army of employees. On entering, a sight met our gaze too revolting to pass from memory. Upon the earthy floor lay two of those sturdy and warm-hearted dwellers of the plains and rockies, cold in death, scalped and mutilated almost beyond recognition—a deed committed by those dastardly red fiends of the far West. Both were friends of mine and with uncovered head, in the presence of that gritty son of old Ireland, I vowed vengeance.

"At least, Charlie," said Patrick, "Let's give them a decent burial and move on."

We did so, reaching camp that evening just as the sun, with its beautiful tints of carmine, was bidding plains and hills goodnight, as if in memory of those stalwart and brave men who made the settlement and civilization of the West possible.

Chapter 7

A Plucky German

Two weeks later a strapping six-foot German, who was in charge of another camp further down the line, came for a visit. Shortly after his arrival, he proposed that we should go hunting, to which I agreed.

That morning, as usual, the men called for their liquor, and among them was a long lanky fellow with red hair and bushy beard. He certainly had the appearance of an outlaw. He had received one glass of grog and came for the second which I refused him. Without a word I was on my back. At that point the German came in and caught him with the left hand in the same locality. Suffering with pain and crazed with liquor, he left the store, secured his revolvers and returned. I was behind the counter at the time with my back to the door. The first thing I knew I heard the report of a revolver and a bullet whizzed past my ear and buried itself in a can of tomatoes not six inches from my head. As I turned around, I saw the fellow being propelled through the door by the German's right. At that point the contractor came in and after being told of what had happened, he discharged the fellow. He wished to retain his revolvers, but his request was not granted. He had an old-fashioned army musket and begged to be allowed to keep that. I told Mr. A—— not to let him have it for I was satisfied from the blow he gave me that he was a bad actor; but Mr. A——, being good natured and kind hearted, consented. He ordered four days' rations put up for him and he left camp in an ugly mood and was given no further thought.

After grub, the German proposed that we flip a coin to see who should go for the horses. The visitor losing, he at once started for the canyon below where the horses were grazing. Shortly after I heard a shot and then many more, but gave it no heed as it was a common occurrence there. Half an hour later one of the men came in and told me that the German lay dead in the canyon below. I, with the others in camp, proceeded to the point indicated, where we found the poor fellow lying on his back. A bullet from that villain's musket had pierced his heart. His watch, belt of cartridges, revolvers, and repeating carbine were gone. After we returned with the body, Mr. A—— had the mill whistle blown calling all hands to quarters and for three days and nights with little sleep or rest we searched those hills and trails leading to Salt Lake and Denver. We picketed men on each trail to search all passing trains; but the demon gave us the slip, and cheated that maddened crowd of a lynching, or something worse; perhaps a tug of war between two wild broncos, which we had in camp, with that man's body as the connecting link.

I can to this day remember just how that poor fellow looked; cold in death, far from home and loved ones, with no mother to weep at his bier. With uncovered heads we lowered him in earth, in a rough box, at the foot of one of the tall sentinels of the hills, and placed a slab to mark the spot, that his friends might some day claim all that remained of as brave and honest a German as ever lived.

A Watchful Providence

Thus by the toss of a coin was my life again spared. This last narrow escape from death was the fourteenth of which I positively knew, and how many more that I did not know of, it is impossible to tell; so I made up my mind to get out of the country alive, if possible. I informed Mr. A—— of my intentions and the following day closed my business and at dusk that evening I started, unaccompanied, on a two hundred mile ride over a trail watched by hundreds of blood-thirsty Indians. I knew that no Indian pony could overtake my fleet runner, and all that was to be feared was a surprise or have my horse shot from under me. I camped far from the trail, with lariat fastened to my wrist, never closing my eyes until my faithful animal had laid down for the day. His first move at dusk awoke me, and, after feed, we were off with the wind at breakneck speed.

At the close of the second day, while I lay sleeping on the desert sands with the saddle blanket for a pillow, and dreaming of my far away home, it seemed as if something of a slimy nature was slowly crawling over the calf of my bare leg. On gaining partial consciousness, too quickly did I realize that it was a reality and not a dream. A rattlesnake's long slimy body was crossing that bridge of flesh, squirming along for a couple of inches, then raising its repulsive body a foot or more and turning its insignificant head, would look straight towards my partly closed eyes and, with its hideous mouth agap, would dart its poisonous arrow-like tongue in and out like lightning, then lowering itself, it would resume the same tactics as before. How many times it repeated this, I shall never know. No words have ever been formed that can adequately express the feeling that took possession of me. I seemed powerless to move a muscle or twitch an eyelid. The suspense was terrible, expecting each time that the slimy body descended the viper would thrust his poisonous lance into my leg and all would be over. The horror of it all cannot be imagined, and to this day, when I recall the incident, it sends a shiver through my entire body. As the coarse rattles of his tail left the bare flesh of my leg, my senses seemed to return; but it was only for a moment, for through the pant of my right leg I felt that same crawling sensation and I knew in an instant that it was a mate following the one that had just passed over the bridge of flesh. As soon as it reached the bare leg the dirty reptile went through the same horrible stunts as the first one. The agony seemed impossible to bear and when at last the thing had completed its journey and was at a safe distance away, I leaped into the air—how far I shall leave the reader to surmise. Crazed with anger and trembling from head to foot, I rushed for my revolvers and fired at random. I was considered a good shot in those days, but in this excited condition I would not have been able to hit a barn. I ran for my Henry Carbine and, grasping it by the barrel, made short work of ridding the earth of the cause that had produced the most terrifying scare experience during my western life.

The Faithful Horse

For the first time during the excitement my thoughts turned to my faithful horse, but he was nowhere to be seen. The horror of the situation began to dawn upon me and I realized at once that I was lost on that desolate plain—one hundred miles from any camp that I knew of and apparently alone. I cried out, "My God, what can be done!"

The thought was enough to drive one crazy. Can I ever forget it? I think not; nor could anyone. Even to see or

Billie! Billie!

talk to an Indian would have been a comfort. Driven to agonizing despair I ran for my field glass and scanned the rolling ground in every direction. Buffalo, deer, antelope, coyote, and a small party of horsemen were visible, but the latter too far away to make out if they were United States Cavalrymen or Indians. Looking again, without my glass, I discovered my horse standing on a high knoll not more than a half mile away with head and tail erect; the breath from his dilated nostrils ascending heavenward in the cold October air and presenting a picture for an artist. I called loudly, "Billie, Billie," and with outstretched hand walked slowly toward him, but he looked not in my direction.

All of a sudden he made a quick bound and was off. My heart seemed to stop beating. A minute seemed an hour; but I kept walking after him and he finally stopped, turned around and faced me. That look can never be forgotten. With ears thrown back, he came slowly toward me. Again, I called "Billie, Billie," and held out both hands and with a whinner he came on a gallop, trembling in every muscle, seemingly as frightened as myself. I patted his neck, straightened out his rich heavy mane, rubbed his face and nose and kissed him. He licked my cheek and hand in appreciation of my welcome; moisture gathered in his large eyes and I cried with joy—like a child that I was—and then we both felt better. I coiled up the lariat and placed my right arm over his perfectly formed neck and slowly walked to our little camp. I rubbed him down until he was perfectly dry; then curried, brushed and rubbed until I could almost see myself in his coat of silky hair. Then I made him lay down and did the same thing myself, using his withers and mane for a pillow. When I awoke the moon shown full in our faces. I patted his neck and soon those large eyes were looking affectionately into mine. I sprang to my feet and he did the same. After brushing off the side on which he had laid, I placed the saddle blanket, buckled taut the saddle, gathered up my small camp kit and fastened it to the rear of the saddle, coiled the lariat and hung it on the pommel of the saddle, fastened on my spurs—from which he had never felt even the slightest touch—threw my field glass over my left shoulder, buckled on my cartridge belt and revolvers, swung my canteen and Henry Carbine over my right shoulder, and with a leap, landed astride the saddle, and was off with the wind in search of the trail two full miles away.

THE INDIANS CAPTURE A FRIEND

Early on the morning of the third day, I stopped at a stage station, where I met the assistant wagon boss who was with the bull train during my first trip across the plains. He was a genuine Missouri Bushwacker and a desperate fellow. Like all others of his class he wore his hair long, making it a much coveted prize for the Indians. After the days visit and relating our experience of western life, he told me that he was on his way to the Black Hills. I reluctantly volunteered the information to him that I did not think he would ever reach there on the old skate he was riding, and that he should not venture on the trail until after dark, but he knew it all and started at sundown. I was sure the fellow would never reach the Hills, nor was I mistaken, for in less than an hour the Salt Lake Coach rolled up to the door of the station, and the driver asked if a horseman had put up at the place, and being informed that there had, told us the Indians had captured him and tied him to one of their own ponies and was rapidly going north, leaving his old nag to be picked up by any one who would care for it. Not a day passed that the unwelcome savages were not to be seen, and we were chased many times, but the faithful animal reached Denver in safety.

The Union Pacific railroad had then reached Julesburg and I conceived the hazardous idea of reaching that point by navigating the Platte River—a distance of three hundred miles—so I at once ordered a flat bottomed boat built of material in the rough.

A Cunning Schemer

I next went in quest of my aged chum, the ex-pig dealer, who, when found, revealed by a twinkle in his eye another dare-devil scheme, which he was quite capable of concocting when alone in his warehouse den. He exclaimed, with much feeling and a forced tear, that he was right down glad to see me safely back and gave me little rest until I had related my experiences in the hills. He then unfolded his diabolical scheme, whereby both of us could lay a foundation for a fortune. I was in need of the latter, without any question, but not by this method.

Cheyenne had just been surveyed, mapped and laid out, and the proposition was for him to furnish a man, two mule teams, wagons, tents, provisions and all other necessities; and this man and myself were to go there and squat or take possession of two sections of government land, consisting of one hundred and sixty acres each, located just outside the city limits. The offer was promptly rejected, and it destroyed the last particle of friendship that had existed between us as far as I was concerned. I had just been through that part of the country and had narrowly escaped death many times, and for us to carry out this scheme, I knew would be impossible, for the tricky redskins would be certain to capture us. I cannot recollect the exact reply that I made him, but am positive I requested him to go to Hades by the shortest possible route. We parted in anger after three long years of friendship. The old major's love for the almighty dollar was the cause. I never did have a very

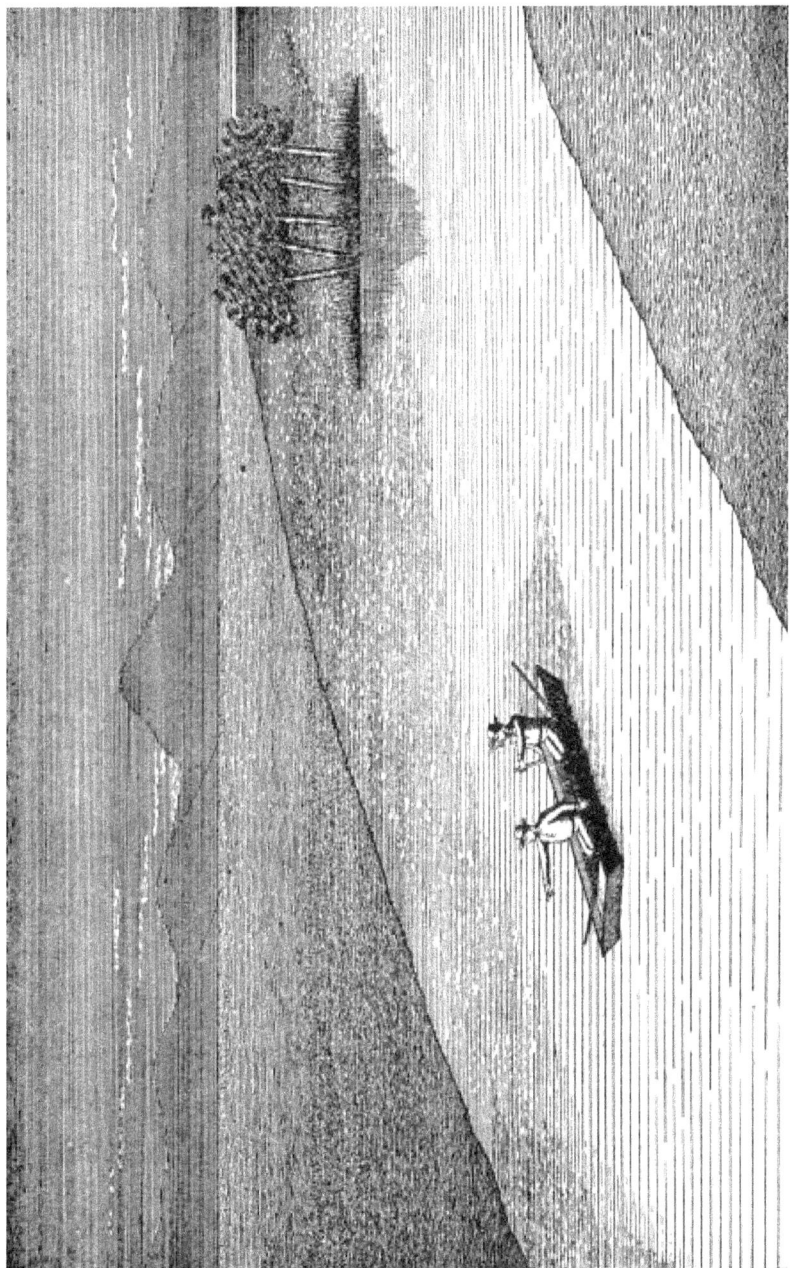

HOME RIDE DOWN THE PLATTE RIVER

strong desire to furnish material to the cruel savages for one of their home scalp dances, and besides my mind was made up to leave Colorado, which I did.

I afterwards made the acquaintance of a young fellow, a college graduate who had been unable to secure a position to his liking and was anxious to return to the States. After a few days of good fellowship, and finding him of the right material, I made my plans known to him. He at once fell in with them, and a week later we embarked on our perilous journey. We started at full moon drifting with a comparatively strong current using paddles to guide our roughly constructed craft. We made nightly rides of about fifty miles, and at dawn would land on one of the small islands of the river, conceal ourselves and the boat in the tall grass from which we were able to see all that passed by trail and bluffs, and not be seen ourselves. Our greatest danger was in being discovered by the Indians on the high bluffs, or a visit from them to the island we occupied. The first scare we had was when a party of a dozen or more rode to the bank of the river for the purpose, as we supposed, of crossing. They seemed, however, undecided as to their course, but finally urged their ponies down the bank and into the river. To describe our feelings would be impossible. Just then, to us, a minute seemed an hour. Cold beads of perspiration stood out on both, not exactly from fear, but a sort of yearning to be elsewhere; and I wondered, after all that I had passed through, if I was to be cut down on my homeward journey by those fiendish red devils. "Saved!" whispered my friend, "they are leaving the river." And sure enough those little prairie ponies were climbing the bank on a dead run for the bluffs.

The last night of that eventful ride lasted long until after the sun was up. The large Concord coach filled with passengers passed close to the river bank a short time before, and from the driver we learned we were ten miles from Julesburg. We proceeded, keeping close to the bank, and with field glass continually swept the valley and bluffs in every direction. We were facing a mild and depressing wind. All of a sudden dismal sounds reached our ears, and as the noiseless current of the river rounded the projecting points in its banks, it bore our staunch old craft to a place of safety, or ourselves to a cruel death, we knew not which. The sounds became more distinct until both of us were satisfied that the Indians had captured the overland coach with its load of human freight. As we rounded the next bend the river took a straight course, but there was no island in sight.

"No island in sight," said my friend. "Where can we go?" And turning around I discovered he was as white as a sheet. As for myself, I was hanging to the edge of the bank trying hard to collect my wits and recover from a fainting spell. We finally managed to get the boat back and around the bend where we lay concealed for some time, suffering the torture of Hades. I finally crawled to the top of the bank and with field glass surveyed the locality in every direction. No life was visible, still the unearthly noise kept up, and the feeling of those two lone travellers would be impossible to describe. The thought at last came to me that we must be somewhere in the vicinity of the old California Crossing. I crawled back to the boat and told my companion to go ahead, while I continually used the field glass. After fifteen minutes, I discovered a white speck in the eastern horizon. We were soon over our fright, and with light hearts were sailing over the rippling waters of the old Platte feeling assured that we would soon reach a place of safety, as far as the Indians were concerned.

On arriving at the crossing, which it proved to be, we found one of those large white covered prairie schooners stalled in the middle of the stream, and fifty Greasers, as the Mexican drivers were called, and as many yoke of oxen trying to haul it out.

Farewell to the Plains

We sailed merrily along and at two p.m. reached Julesburg, the then terminus of the Union Pacific railroad and overland shipping point for all territory west, north and south. The Union Pacific railroad, when under construction, made a terminus every two or three hundred miles. The houses were built in sections, so they were easily taken apart, loaded on flat freight cars, and taken to the next terminus completely deserting the former town, Julesburg was rightfully named "The Portable Hell of the Plains." My finer feelings cannot, if words could, attempt a description. Suffice to say that during the three days we were there four men and women were buried in their street costumes. The fourth day we boarded a Union Pacific train and were whirled to its Eastern terminus, Omaha, thence home, arriving safely after an absence of four years.

The habits formed during those western years were hard to change, and the fight of my life to live a semblance of the proper life, required a will power as irresistible as the crystal quartz taken from the lofty snow capped mountain sides, taking tons of weight to crush it, that the good might be separated from the worthless.

The Story of a Pioneer

Yours Truly
V. Deverany

To the Brave Pioneers and their Children

My Friends and Comrades

who reclaimed from savagery and dreary desolation
the great desert region of the West, and converted it
into a home of enlightened civilization and wealth,
this book is affectionately dedicated with pride and
pleasure by

The Author

Acknowledgements

For appreciated assistance in the publication of this work the author is indebted to the following persons: For endorsement of its merits and urging its publication, to Mr. C. A. Bonfils, editor of the *Sunday Post*, a paper popular by force of its worth. For art work to Mr. F. E, Graf. For valuable suggestions and approval to Mrs. Adda A. Stanley and Isalene B. Reed. Also to my publisher, for so neatly dressing up my thoughts in the beauties of the typographic art. All of which are hereby gratefully acknowledged.

Preface

The remarkable events and circumstances in connection with the exciting rush of 1859-60 to Pike's Peak, the only point then known and named near the reported rich gold fields of Colorado, should be indelibly impressed upon the minds of the people as a heritage and memorial of the admirable and heroic work of the brave pioneers. Their grand and glorious work has won our gratitude and respect. In the land of the hostile Indian and the wild beast he built his home, and risked his life, his health and his fortune to subdue it and make it prolific.

To revive and preserve in memory the heroic deeds of the pioneer, who is now fast passing away, and to relate some of the peculiar occurrences, and portray a few of the grotesque scenes in connection therewith, is my pride, privilege and purpose in this narrative.

Never again will the same primitive conditions and circumstances be seen or re-enacted within the wide borders of these United States, for the wild grandeur of the scenes in this once vast desert plain has been destroyed. The quiet repose of beast and bird has been disturbed, or they have become extinct. The enterprise of man and the railroad have entered into all the wild places of the Great West, and opened them up to civilization. The buffalo and Indian no longer roam the plains; the stately elk and the fleet-footed antelope no longer make a living picture against the pale blue sky; nor does the heavy freight wagon drawn by six yoke of oxen or five span of mules, steer its way over the hills and prairies.

No more is the long emigrant train seen wearily wending its way over the hills and valleys of the plains; but in its stead the railway locomotive with its piercing voice and thundering sound shoots over it. The rugged and attractive scenes of nature in her undisturbed beauty have passed away. Never again will the spirit of man find a welcoming echo in the wild hills and the vast, silent prairies, for it was the fate of the pioneer to destroy the beauty that charmed him. While it is not for those who come after him to see and feel this wild grandeur, still they may catch a glimpse of it in *The Story of a Pioneer*.

Yours Truly
T. Devinny

Edgewater
Colorado

Beautiful Colorado!
  The fairest of the fair.
With brilliant sun
  And crystal air.
And farms, and mines,
  Of richest worth—
The choicest place
  For homes on earth.

Introduction

The conversion of the plains of the far West, once known as the Great American Desert, into a suitable abode for civilized man was a peculiarly grand and wonderful work for the brave and heroic pioneer. This development was due, in a great measure, to the immense immigration which poured into the gold fields of Colorado in the spring of 1860 and subsequent years. The people who entered into this expedition boldly risked life and all that was dear to them in their long, perilous and tedious journey by wagon train over the arid plains, then occupied by savage Indians and wild beasts.

The thrilling scenes and incidents encountered in connection with the peculiar life and travel upon the plains and through the mountains on that memorable occasion, which were experienced by myself and by the author of this book, as well, furnish ample material, when property collated and arranged, for a highly interesting and pleasing narrative.

It affords me, therefore, much pleasure to learn that the author has taken upon himself the commendable task of making a connected and reliable narrative of these strange and wonderful incidents of the then wild and undeveloped West, of which I believe him in every way capable, and whom I have the honour to claim as my last and most efficient instructor in the days of my boyhood.

W. F. Cody
"Buffalo Bill"

It seems but a just tribute to the heroism of these early pioneers to properly place upon record the striking incidents which led to and resulted in the transformation of the great desert region of the West into a veritable Garden of Eden, dotted with farms, homes, towns and cities, where dwell a prosperous and happy people, thus furnishing and transmitting to the future historian the peculiar conditions and wild surroundings now destroyed by advancing civilization, and now no more to be seen by mortal eye, under which by the genius of man, the dreary desert was awakened from its dead slumber of centuries by the inspiring waters of irrigation, which the thirsty soil of the desert eagerly drank, and lo and behold! it bloomed and blossomed as the rose. The hidden treasures of the mountains were then also opened up, and thus the desert region was made one of the richest and most attractive of the earth.

I am glad to encourage the author in his pleasant rehearsal of these stirring incidents, so familiar to both of us, furnishing as it does a pen-picture of the wonderful transformation of the wild waste lands of the West into a marvellously productive region, supplying all the wants and comforts of civilized man.

Cody
Wyoming
March, 1904

The Story of a Pioneer

The rush to the gold regions of Colorado in the spring of 1860 was most remarkable. The lives of those brave pioneers, were fraught with many interesting incidents, which, if collected, would form a treasure store, descriptive of the conquests, pain, perils and shattered hopes attending western pioneer life. It stirs to admiration and inspires the mind with noble feelings to contemplate the heroism of the pioneer settlers of a new country who leave relatives and friends and the dear homes of their childhood to dwell upon the western prairie—wild, cheerless and undeveloped—away from all that is dear to head and heart, there to build new cities and new homes, and form new ties of friendship.

Those who, at this period, witnessed these vast trains of moving wagons, drawn by mules, horses, oxen, and even by cows, or beheld the less fortunate travelling with hand carts loaded with "bed and board," and footmen with packs upon their backs—as motley and as strange a procession as ever eye beheld, five or more miles long—could not but have entertained feelings experienced by these travellers. It was a sight never to be forgotten—this vast caravan, moving slowly along in the distance, over hilltop and plain, forming a dark, curving line across the far-reaching green prairie, like a monster serpent in its slow-travelling search for food.

The life of a pioneer is not, as many suppose, a life of

pleasant adventure and delightful romance; on the contrary, it is one of stern reality, demanding the full and complete action of both the mental and physical qualities of man—full of responsibility, toil and care.

Among the vast number of people who sought gain and gold in Colorado at this early date there were but few families. Many married men, it is true, made their way here, but with but few exceptions, they wisely left their families behind. The greater portion were unmarried men of various ages in search of fickle fortune's favour.

It is not the purpose of this narrative to record the good fortune or failures of those numberless adventurers, nor to describe the good results or benefits to the now-grand state of Colorado in consequence of this great rush to the Pike's Peak gold region.

One family, however, whose neat and well equipped wagon formed one of this great train, was drawn by two beautiful black horses, impatient under the enforced restraint, incident to the tardy progress of the slow-moving train of wagons in advance of them. Their wagon, like the others, was loaded with provisions, blankets, cooking utensils and other requisites of camp life. Its occupants consisted of four persons, Mr. and Mrs. Neal Norton, their fair daughter Nora, and her uncle, Andrew Norton, whom Nora familiarly termed Uncle "Drew."

The Nortons were intelligent, well-to-do farm people, who had taken a claim on government land in western Kansas, but receiving a fair offer for it, sold it, and being influenced by highly coloured and exaggerated stories of the recent discovery of rich mines of gold in Cherry Creek, they "fixed up" and joined the train bound for Pike's Peak.

Pike's Peak was then the only point named and known in that vast, wild, arid region, and though seventy-five miles from the point of discovery of gold on Cherry Creek—

now the present site of Denver—yet it gave a name for a time at least to the gold region of Colorado, in the midst of what was then described in the geographies as the Great American Desert, but which is now better known as western Kansas, Nebraska, Colorado, Montana and Idaho. Although it is a region with an insufficiency of rainfall in summer, it is not, in any sense, a desert, nor can it be called a plain, for Idaho, Montana and a part of Colorado are very mountainous regions.

The trip from Leavenworth, Kansas, the then frontier town, over the plains to Cherry Creek, a distance of about six hundred miles, and completed in six weeks' time, was a pleasant one to the members of this great caravan. The weather was warm and pleasant, for it was in the merry months of May and June. The thick, velvety grass formed on the almost treeless landscape a beautiful carpet of brightest green. The bright sun poured down in its wonted way a continuous flood, of soft, silvery, sparkling light, peculiar to this region, from a never-varying cloudless sky. This, together with the clear, colourless air, always void of smoke or fog, gave to the whole scene a weird, electric-light-like tint.

There was another strange peculiarity of the atmospheric condition of the plains which occasioned much wonder. There appeared day after day for several weeks, far in the distance, ahead of the train, dim but distinct views of real forests, sometimes spires and towers were also seen for a time, then all would fade away to appear again the next day perhaps, like the in-coming and out-going scenes of a magic lantern. This incomprehensible phenomenon was always a bewildering mystery, giving cause for many a discussion or queer explanation. The forests, steeples and towers, faded away as we approached them. The explanation of this interesting illusion is, that the dry air, heated by the intense sunshine of the plains, rising in undulating waves, lifts up, and spreads out, and magnifies the lines of vision coming from the object seen—magnified or distorted, and thus carried to the eye of the beholder. Thus shapely weeds, not a foot high, are by this condition of the atmosphere, converted into tall, well proportioned trees or forests; and in like manner stumps of weeds into towers or citadels, and tall spears of grass are magnified into pinnacles or steeples.

The few feathered songsters, the occasional wild flowers, the absence of trees and shrubbery, the few antelope and buffalo seen—for they had receded from the line of travel on the approach of man—and the general absence of life all around, caused a sense of loneliness and gloom to creep into one's mind, and bring up brighter scenes of home and happy friends far away. But those who travel by team and wagon have little time to give to gloomy thoughts, however much they may amuse or interest. The excitement and work of travel, and the watchfulness necessary in an Indian country, leave little time for aught else. The distance travelled was but fifteen or twenty— seldom twenty-five— miles per day, so as to reach "good camping ground." That is to say, where there was grass and water for the teams, and fuel for the camp fire. As the line of travel pursued was on the old California trail of '49, along and up the valley of the Platte River, these requisites were always found; fuel from the scrubby willows on its moist banks, water from its channel and grass along its borders.

A natural feeling of loneliness and a want of protection inspires one with a desire for companionship and association, hence this vast train was held together and controlled by a sort of influence of its own. The action of the few was the action of all. As a swarm of bees follows the leader, and as all nestle upon the same branch she alights upon, so in this case when the leaders of the train turned out of the

BEAUTIFUL NORA NORTON
THE VICTIM OF MISFORTUNE—THE QUEEN OF WEALTH

road toward camping ground, the others followed under a natural law of association, each selecting a choice spot upon which to pitch his tent, or stand his wagon, or upon which to cast his saddle and blankets, and graze his horse, if a horseman.

This done, the scene then presented was grand and peculiar. All was life and bustle. Like children just out from school, the newly made camp was all astir. There was running hither and thither, some to the river for water, some for willow brush for the camp fire, while others with spoon, pan and flour were preparing to compound the historic "slap-jack" of camp life. For travel sharpens the appetite and

119

gives flavour to, and even makes delicious, the plainest sort of food, so that meal-time was a most important event.

In a very short time the simple meal is ready, and placed on a blanket or table linen spread out upon the green grass, around which all gather and seat themselves on the ground, after the fashion and manner of a tailor, while the few women had a manner of their own—dropping on their knees, and making a seat of their dainty feet. All is gay and festive now; pleasant odours of the recently prepared meal float upon the air; merry voices ring out, and the joyous laugh is heard throughout the camp. The scene presented to the eye of a beholder is truly magnificent!

A city of white canvas-covered wagons and tents, stretched out along the river, with horses, mules and cattle grazing between, in the midst of a green sea-like prairie, with its citizens in this queer posture, engaged in taking their noon-day meal, with the blue smoke from the now smouldering camp fires lazily ascending toward a cloudless sky of purest blue, from which poured forth over all, through the thin, colourless, glistening air, a flood of crystal light—this was the scene presented, and the manner of travel of those hardy pioneers, day after day, as they boastfully paraded in crude letters on their wagon covers, the motto, "Bound for Pike's Peak," or "For the Gold Diggings."

To break the monotony of travel and camp life, field sports, fishing, hunting and shooting were frequently resorted to. As sailors upon long sea voyages, to while away the dullness of time, resort to story telling, so the travellers on the sea-like prairie engaged in song and story, as they squatted in circles around their weak, blazing camp fires. Many a good story was thus told, and many a song was sung. Mutual dependence and reliance, one upon the other, for aid or benefit, engenders confidence and friendship the world over.

Hence a feeling of trust and esteem naturally bind frontiersmen together forming a union of fellowship and tenderness which is seldom forgotten. Friendships were thus formed around the camp fires and on the road which endured as long and were as dear as life itself.

The Nortons, with their attractive "outfit," drew around them many genial and admiring friends, who always camped near them, and thus were in one sense companions and neighbours. The camp fire of the Nortons was generally made large enough to enable all their friends to cook their food over its flames. On these occasions it was the joy and delight of little Nora to assist in the work of the camp. She brought the water from the river, while her mother made ready the cooking utensils for the expectant campfire meal. Being the only child in that part of the long train, her busy nature and lithesomeness made her a conspicuous and notable little personage throughout the camp. Her deportment and warm, genial manner added much to her attractiveness. Her every-day salutations to strangers and friends fell from her lips, wreathed in circles of smiles, as readily and pleasantly as notes from a sweet song bird. Her bright, cheerful face was an unfailing index to the joy and content which filled her mind. Petty crosses and disappointments which so often trouble others never found their way through the sunshine of her heart. She was, at this time, of stout, rather short build, and but fifteen years of age. Her features were regular and well formed, her complexion neither dark nor fair, but merged into both. Her hair was jet black, falling in loose, wavy lines to her shoulders. Her eyes, dark and sparkling, stood out prominently, while her full, red lips, firmly set, displayed much self reliance. She had a clear-cut nose, somewhat of the Grecian type. Her features, taken as a whole, were indicative of fine mental powers and great possibilities.

As previously stated, Nora's father and mother were industrious, intelligent country people, who felt the necessity of inculcating into the minds of the young the importance of knowledge, industry and business ability, which manifested itself in the characteristics of their only daughter. Aside from this they possessed no marked quality in form or feature materially differing from many other respectable men and women one meets in the every day walks of life.

But Andrew Norton—"Uncle Drew"—requires more than passing notice. As a child, he was self-willed and insubordinate, and caused his mother, then a widow, much trouble and anxiety. But feeling that this needful restraint was an abuse, after a reprimand for a serious disobedience, he stole away from the home of his childhood, and was not heard from, for ten long years. Then a short letter came to his mother from him postmarked California, from which she gleaned little regarding his business or manner of life. After ten more years of mysterious silence he returned home to see his old mother, his total absence from home being twenty years. His aged and feeble mother, overjoyed at seeing him, fell upon his neck with sobs and tears. She could not control her troubled heart. She felt the ingratitude of her son in forgetting, for so many long years, his duty to his mother, whose affectionate solicitude for him in helpless infancy, gave to her many a weary day, and stole from her, many a much-needed night's rest, and thus, in a measure, he owed her a vast debt of gratitude, for she was the watchful attendant of his life, and the guardian of it through the helplessness of infancy. While she felt in its fullness the depth of the wrong she had suffered, yet, with a mother's undying love for her offspring, she rejoiced that she again beheld her long-lost son.

The meeting was of too exciting a nature for her in her feeble condition, and in less than a fortnight its effect was noticeable. She grew less active and weaker day by day, and thus gradually she faded till death stole in and hushed her to sleep—blessed sleep, that closed the dreamer's eyes to the ingratitude and baseness of this vain world.

Before her death Drew learned that his brother Neal and family resided in western Kansas, whither he went in search of them after he had weepingly followed the remains of his aged mother to the tomb.

He arrived just in time to find his brother and family on the eve of leaving their farm, and joined them in their western journey. He gave them much valuable advice and assistance in the selection of the many needful things for the long journey. It required considerable thought and judgment to properly load the wagon, which is a small affair to hold the necessary things for a journey, and leave room for the family besides. Provisions are of first importance, and there must be an abundance. Clothing, bedding, tableware and cooking utensils, all must find a place.

There was one incident in loading the wagon deserving mention, which was beneficent in its ultimate results to Nora Norton at least, and it proves also how little things reach out into the impenetrable future and affect our lives for good or evil. In collecting together the household goods it became evident that the trunks and boxes on hand were insufficient to hold them. So Nora, in a merry mood, said:

"I'll pack my things in that ten-gallon dairy can."

This was done. Her "things" consisted of a few toilet articles and a limited wardrobe.

Dairy cans have iron bottoms, both to save them from wear and also to serve, like the ballast in a ship, to keep them upright in a rolling dairy wagon.

Andrew Norton claimed Pike's Peak was on his way home, and he would, therefore, be glad to accompany them and assist in their search for gold for a few weeks at least;

after which he said he must proceed to his more important business. But he seemed guarded in his conversation relative to his business affairs and occupation. He appeared to be possessed of considerable means, had plenty of ready money, spent it freely, and seemed content and happy. He was of medium height, with uncut hair. Like the hunters and trappers of that day, he wore a buckskin suit, decorated with beaver fur, and a brown hat, with a band of beaver fur. This, together with his bronzed face and long beard, stamped him as a trapper or hunter.

Be this as it may, he never gave any explanation relative to his odd garb, except to say it was the fashion of the people on the frontier where he dwelt.

He was familiar with western manners, ways and methods, and prolific in frontier stories, with which he delighted the campfire circle, thus charming away the dreary dullness which 50 often gathered around it. On one occasion, while thus engaged, little Nora came rushing into camp, which was in the vicinity of old Fort Kearney, on the Platte river, and with that earnest excited manner peculiar to childhood, said:

"Oh, father, I saw some people asleep in the tops of those cottonwood trees yonder!" pointing to a clump of scrubby trees.

"Yes," replied her Uncle Drew, "I guess they are in their last sleep, and will never awaken."

"Why, Uncle Drew! What do you mean? They must be asleep, because they are wrapped snugly in their blankets, and I could see they were resting easy, on cross pieces well secured to opposite branches."

"That is doubtless true," replied her Uncle Drew, "for I think what you describe are Indian graves, and the wrappings you saw were the only shroud and coffin of the dead."

"Why, how queer," said Nora musingly. "To think that people would bury their friends in a tree top!"

Then addressing her uncle, she said:

"Why don't they bury their dead in the ground?"

"Because," replied her uncle, "they have no tools with which to dig graves, and if they did, the half-starved coyotes would dig them up and eat them, hence they envelope their dead in buffalo robes or blankets, and securely fasten them in a tree top, beyond their reach. But out on the treeless prairie, from sheer necessity, they do dig a shallow grave with their hatchets and hands and bury their dead therein, leaving them there to be forever forgotten."

A visit to the clump of trees designated verified the surmises of Nora's uncle, for several dead bodies were seen in the tree-tops enveloped as described, and firmly lashed to the branches of the trees with cords of rawhide. A well lettered notice put up by the Indian agent warned all persons not to molest the graves. As no Indians had been seen up to this time, these graves were the first indication that we were then in an Indian country, and with many there was much curiosity to see Indians in their native haunts, and to behold "the noble red man," as described in works of fiction, "in his unadorned beauty." Others, with less courage, shuddered at the thought of seeing an Indian. But we did not have long to wait to see these curious denizens of the plains, for the next day we located near an Indian camp, and we were afforded ample opportunity to observe the peculiarities of Indian home-life. But the glamour which filled our fancy with bright and pleasant thoughts was quickly dispelled on first sight of these dusty, dirty people. Their dress was neither neat nor clean. Old, castaway clothing of various colours, shapes and fits, tattered and torn, and blankets and buffalo robes drawn economically around them, hid their unwashed bodies from sight, and shielded them from the cold, chilling winds of winter and the scorching suns of summer.

It is true, however, that chiefs and their sons, and other favourites of the tribe, have a gaudy display dress, beaded and feathered, for special occasions, but these are the exceptions and not the rule.

Their cookery, or rather want of it, is so at variance with any reasonably conceived idea of it, as to be incredible, except to those who have witnessed it. The raw flesh of animals they cut into long, narrow strips, and wrap it in a spiral form around a green, straight branch, or stick, and in its unwashed state hold it, not over, but in, the blaze of their camp fires till roasted. When cool enough to do so, they place its end in the side of their mouths, and munch it like a dog, unrolling it by turning the stick as they consume it. If the supply of meat is limited, they cut the entrails into suitable lengths, pass them between their compressed finger and thumb, to empty them of their contents, and, in their unwashed state, without more ado, they wrap them around the stick and proceed to cook them in the manner previously stated. Their food is often of the most disgusting nature. Grasshoppers and worms, unwashed and uncooked reptiles are eaten by them with a relish astonishing to behold. Their reputed skill as marksmen, and their reputation for agility and strength, all vanish before the face of truth. They are both uncouth and clumsy, and the scene they present on horseback is truly grotesque. The highly-coloured stories of the nobility of the red man, and the gilded character given to the wild Indian, have no foundation in fact, existing only in the fancy of the writers of fiction, who use them to adorn their tales. When the train arrived in the vicinity of Julesburg—then but a stage station—a highly exciting incident occurred. The train had camped for the day near some trains *en-route* for Salt Lake City with supplies. All was quiet in camp. The noonday meal was past. Some were telling stories, some repairing harness or washing clothes; others were asleep or resting in the shadow of their wagons. All of a sudden a monster buffalo, lost from his herd, came prancing toward and into camp, his long, massive mane, covering shoulders, neck and forehead, undulated at every step as he advanced. The alarm was given by someone as he approached, and in an instant guns, revolvers and even knives were gotten out, and the camp was soon filled with excitement and confusion. Shooting at the animal began from every direction, but he was neither killed nor turned from his course, for his heavy mane was to him a protecting shield. He was soon in the midst of camp, when the most intense excitement prevailed, and the most reckless and dangerous shooting was engaged in, for as the people gathered in a circle around the beast, the balls missing him would strike the opposite side of the circle. Fortunately, none were hurt, but the buffalo, maddened by the flesh wounds he had received, dashed furiously through the camp, trampling over tin pans, kettles and other camp utensils, and scattering the frightened people in every direction. He started off toward the river in a loping run, from which Nora Norton was then seen to be returning.

Maddened and crazed with pain as he then was, all felt that poor Nora was doomed, and a piteous cry was heard throughout the camp, as her perilous position was realized. Her mother fainted from fright, while her father and uncle cried aloud in deepest agony. As nearer and nearer the enraged animal approached her the suspense and excitement became almost unendurable, for the ferocious beast was then, it seemed, but a few rods from her. But just at this exciting moment, a well-grown boy with gun in hand was seen going toward Nora in a rapid run. Hope filled the hearts of all for a moment, but it was soon to be dispelled, for the young man was not an instant by her side before he was seen to run as rapidly away to the right of the line pursued by the beast. Then suddenly wheeling round, he raised his gun to his shoulder with the skill of a trained marksman and fired, and the monster beast fell dead, pierced to the heart by a bullet.

Nora stood motionless, for she had become paralyzed with fright when she realized her danger. A joyous shout now filled the air, and a rush of the people of the camp was made toward Nora and her benefactor. Congratulations were then bestowed upon Nora for her wonderful escape from so terrible a death, while upon her rescuer were showered praise and thanks in no unstinted measure. He was so modest that the praise bestowed upon him for this heroic act overwhelmed him with confusion. He explained that he receded from the side of Nora to take aim at the heart of the beast, well knowing that a bullet could never reach his brain through nature's shield—his mane-covered head.

His firm, positive method of speaking, together with his noble bearing, attracted marked attention, and indicated one capable of great possibilities. The young man was then known as Bill Cody, now better known as Colonel William F. Cody, the world famous "Buffalo Bill," and an old-time friend and pupil of the writer.

At this time Colonel Cody was a lithe, slender boy in his teens, and then manifested many of the characteristics which lead him later on to accomplish a notoriety attained by few. His education was limited to "the three R's, reading, 'riting and 'rithmetic," a trio of potent factors, which has enabled many to fill honoured and lucrative places in both private and public life. As a pupil under the author's tutelage in a country schoolhouse, near Leavenworth City, Kansas, his bearing was upright and stately, his movements quick and abrupt, his language decisive and authoritative. While he loved pleasure and play, he was not rompish, nor rude, his manners being modest, dignified and quiet. His deportment was beyond reproach. Collateral to this, his judgment and opinions, even as a boy, were generally good, quickly formed, and determinedly carried out. Illustrative of this, and to show the animus of his mind, the author will relate this incident. One day in the noon-day ball game he shouted to his comrade:

"Don't be all day getting ready to strike, but strike, and strike to hit."

This was so much like the noted declaration of Shakespeare, *"Don't stand on the order of going but go,"* that the author never forgot it. These striking characteristics of his nature gave him pre-eminence in executive, ability and enabled him to triumphantly carry out his undertakings to successful fruition, thus making himself famous the world over.

At this time, although but 15 years old, he was making his second trip across the plains as an ox teamster of one of the freight trains camped near by, and was returning from a hunt when he appeared in the scene just described. The Nortons now seemed transported into a new life, as it were, of joy and delight by the happy termination of this perilous incident. An enlarged feeling of kindness and good will, now seemed to have entered and taken possession of their hearts, for they now felt that God reigns in the hearts of men and that there should exist a feeling of benevolence and good will from one to another. Hence they were observed to have become more cheerful, friendly and pleasant.

Bill Cody and his chum, Enoch Allen, a genteel young man of twenty-one years, were never so welcome as now to a seat beside the camp fire or to a Sunday dinner with the Nortons.

But the tedious journey was soon to end; the destination would be reached in a few days. A cut-off road to the gold diggings on Cherry Creek was now to be taken. Bill Cody and Enoch Allen visited the Nortons to bid them goodbye, for at this point they must take another route, their destination being Salt Lake City. To the Nortons the parting was an affecting one, and so far as is known to the writer it was the last meeting between Bill Cody and Nora Norton.

The next week the train reached Cherry Creek, where the first gold had been washed out of its sands. Upon the banks of the stream a dozen or more mud huts had already been built. To the travel-worn people of the train the prospect for a home or fortune was a sad one. Gold was found in but limited quantities, and in but few places in the sand drifts in the channel of the creek. In no instance was the gold sufficient to pay for washing it out of the vast quantity of sand in which it was found. The ground was dry and sandy and almost destitute of vegetation.

General gloom and disappointment spread through the camp; some denounced the reports as lies, and the reporters as liars and villains; some swore, others prepared with curses on their lips to return the next day. But the major portion of the people of the train scattered out and camped along the clear streams of water in the vicinity, both to rest themselves and to look over the country. There was no general method of doing; each one followed his own inclination in this matter. Some who had gone into the mountains returned for supplies and gave encouraging reports of gold discoveries, exhibiting as proof small nuggets of gold, while others showed fine or grain gold in quills, which formed convenient tubular bottles. This revived the drooping spirits of many and renewed their hopes. The Nortons, after a two weeks' rest, determined to go into the mountains on a prospecting tour. They had learned, however, from members of the train, that their friend, Enoch Allen, had abandoned his purpose of going to Salt Lake City as a teamster and instead had bought a good outfit, and with an old friend for a companion had started into the mountains to prospect for gold. The usual outfit for these excursions into the mountains was a saddle horse and one or two pack animals, mules or donkeys, for transporting the provisions and camp fixtures. Had the Nortons gone into the mountains with an outfit of this sort, instead of a team and wagon, their sad misfortune would, perhaps, never have occurred, nor would this sad story ever have been told. But true it is, that the misfortunes of life are seldom foreshadowed, and, therefore, fall upon us when least expected.

The camp on Cherry Creek had now, after a fortnight, become much reduced. But few wagons and tents were now visible where dozens had been seen but a short time before. The Nortons now began their journey to the mountains, but a few hours' travel distant. They soon reached the foothills which, figuratively speaking, are the baby mountains of the great Rocky Mountain range. Little Nora, and even her father, mother and uncle, were delighted with the grand scene now presented to view. Mountains of incomprehensible magnitude and height reached to the clouds. The solid granite rock, seamed, wrinkled and weather beaten, with sides cracked and torn asunder by the eruptive powers of the intense frost and cold of many winters, and the suns of many summers, adorned as they were with patches of green grass and clumps of bushes, vines and trees, the contemplation of which filled their minds with wonder.

The varied nature of the mountain scenery, its snow-capped peaks, water-cut channels, and crystal springs and streams, its evergreen forests and fragrant flowers, caused

Nora, in an ecstasy of joy, to exclaim: "Oh, father, camp here for a week, for everything is so pretty."

Her father replied: "Daughter, dear, we will have these pretty things, I hope, all through the mountains."

They continued their journey into the mountains, passing through Golden Gate, and following the gulch which has now become the road to Central City. Their progress was necessarily slow, for, though there was a visible trail made by horsemen and pack animals, no wagon as yet had passed over it. Often they were obliged to cut away brush or small trees in order to pass, or to dig away the banks of small streams to pass their wagon through them. Hence they travelled but a few miles a day.

As they advanced, the sides of the mountains bore evidence of the work of some mysterious and powerful force. Trees were seen raggedly cut into, or cut off, as if by a canon ball. Upon closer investigation it was discovered that this was the work of immense rocks, which, loosened by frost, slid from their bases and rolled down the precipitous mountain side with a velocity and force which destroyed everything in their way.

Another striking phenomenon peculiar to the Rocky Mountains, showing the terrible power of the elements, is the heavy, almost pouring rains, termed by mountaineers, "cloudbursts." The rain descends with such rapidity as to form, during its continuance, a sheet of water an inch or more deep over the mountain sides and hilltops, which rapidly flows into the mountain streams and gulches, filling them with turbulent, madly rushing waters, often five or six feet deep; thus forming a dangerous and death-dealing instrument to every living thing in its way.

As our travellers penetrated further into the higher and moister regions of the mountains, vegetation became more rank and the underbrush and trees more abundant, which materially interfered with their progress. The trail now led over a low, smooth mountain into a long, deep gulch, which they concluded to enter. After following this trail for a day they became aware that they were going astray, as indicated by their pocket compass, but they decided to continue in the same course.

In the morning of the next day Uncle Drew, who was a good marksman, shouldered his gun and went in pursuit of some deer seen on the mountain side, saying that he would keep along the top of the mountain, in sight of the wagon. But, alas, how often do our wisest plans and fondest hopes fail! He soon came within gunshot of the deer, but only succeeded in crippling one; for it soon ran away, marking its path with blood. He reloaded his gun and quickly followed the wounded animal, to get another shot, but as he passed near a clump of bushes, he was met face to face with a large she-bear and her young cubs. With a warning, hissing grunt she instantly sprang toward him. Standing on her hind legs, she made a circling stroke with her right paw striking him on the left arm, knocking the half-elevated gun from his hands. The force of her blow was sufficient to knock him down, her sharp claws cutting and lacerating his arm and breast badly. She then seized him by the foot, biting through his boot and sinking her teeth deeply into his flesh. He tried to regain his feet, but could not, nor could he reach his gun, for she held his foot in a vice-like grip between her jaws.

Her cubs, now missing their mother, made a piteous call. Quickly releasing her hold she ran to them, but in a moment turned to renew the attack. Drew had seized his gun in the interval and was now ready to receive her. Taking deliberate aim, he fired, and the huge animal lay at his feet in the throes of death. The cubs, on hearing the report of the gun, took fright and fled.

Weakened from pain and loss of blood, and unable to walk, Drew crept into the shade of a tree, out of the warm July sun, where he lay in an almost senseless state till the morning of the next day. Within an hour after Drew had left his brother and family, a dark, threatening cloud was seen to the right of the gulch in which they were travelling, clearly indicating, by the loud thunder and the bright flashes of lightning darting among the clouds, that a terrible rain or "cloud-burst" was imminent, although the sun was still shining brightly in the gulch, and all about was peace and quiet. Hence they felt no apprehension of danger, for Drew had gone away in the opposite direction, and all was pleasant, with sweet singing birds in the trees and bright coloured flowers in bloom all around.

"Oh, mother," said Nora, 'let me get out of the wagon and gather some of those blue flowers."

Her mother assenting, she was assisted to alight and began ascending the mountain upon which the flowers grew.

Her father drove the wagon quite slowly up the narrow gulch in order to enable her the sooner to overtake them. They had proceeded scarcely forty rods after Nora

THE CLOUD-BURST

left them, when the still narrow gulch made a sharp turn round the corner of a high mountain.

Having made this turn, Nora and her parents were in such a position, with respect to the now intervening mountain, as to be entirely out of sight of each other. Mr. and Mrs. Norton now heard a loud noise, seemingly a short distance from them up the gulch, like the cracking of brush and timber, and a dull, roaring sound like the rushing of a great river. They had no time for reflection, nor for action, for in an instant they saw, but a few rods before them, a sight which appalled them. The gulch had received the collected waters of the heavy rain or "cloud-burst" previously mentioned, and it was rushing rapidly down the steep gulch, four or five feet high, pushing rocks, logs and brush before it. Pent up by the resistance of this debris, and checked in its progress, it would raise itself still higher, break through it and fall forward like a tumbling wall, on whatever it met in its way.

Thus rolling and sweeping, with a roaring sound it came upon these unfortunate people like a mighty ocean wave. Hemmed in on both sides by steep mountains, escape was impossible. The avalanche of debris and water was now nearly upon them. The horses took fright, and becoming unmanageable, turned suddenly around, upsetting the wagon with its occupants. The horses fell, one upon the other, a cry of distress was heard from Nora's parents, and in another instant the deep cruel waters swept over all, burying them from sight forever.

Nora, still busily gathering flowers, knew nothing of the terrible death which her parents had met, so near to her, that but for the pitying arm of the mountain which intervened and hid them from her view she must have witnessed their tragic end.

From her position on the mountain side she heard the

terrific roar of the water, and saw it rushing violently, in immense volumes, down the gulch below.

Seeing this immense stream of water, coming from whence she could not tell, on so clear a day, she became alarmed, and ran up the gulch to find her father and mother whom, alas, she would never see again. She could advance but a short distance, for the mountain sides, in places, were nearly perpendicular, and the gulch was full, from side to side, with the rushing water. Filled with dread and anxiety, she sat down on a rock and wept, for she now feared the worst.

She thus sat, distressed by uncertainty and fear for some time, a melancholy object of pity, overwhelmed by the trouble which oppressed her heart. Arousing herself, however, from the stupor into which she had been cast by the fearful circumstances surrounding her, she observed that the water in the gulch was growing less, and it continued to decrease, till in another hour, it had dwindled down to a small stream. Nora then resumed her search for her parents, but had not gone far when the gulch narrowed and presented such steep, precipitous falls, and was so full of huge scattered rocks that she knew no one could pass them. Then her heart sank within her; but she continued her search, hoping against fate. She noted the changed condition of the gulch. The water had dug away the earth in one place, and formed new banks of sand and earth in another; had filled up hollows and cut away ridges. Excitedly she ran up and down the gulch, shouting for her father, mother and her Uncle Drew in agonized tones of grief and despair.

Less than half a mile below where she had collected the flowers, she made a discovery which overwhelmed her with grief. She found remnants of her father's harness, a wheel of his wagon and a blanket lodged in the bushes and trees in the gulch. She also found the dairy can containing her wardrobe and toilet articles which was strangely caught, and held by the broken limb of a tree, which was run through its handle. It rode upon the turbulent waters like a boat, owing to its iron ballasted bottom.

Listlessly, after examining it and finding her clothes dry, she hid it, scarcely knowing why, in the cavity of a mountain. In a further and more critical search of the gulch, she discovered the feet of one of the horses protruding from a newly formed bank of sand, the body evidently having been covered over in its formation. Remnants of the wagon were in like manner found projecting from another bank of sand, but nowhere did she find any evidence of the position of the bodies of her lost father or mother.

When knowledge of the death of her parents was thus made apparent to her, a sense of the utter helplessness of her situation flashed upon her, and she was overcome by a violent fit of grief from which she could hardly free herself.

But the buoyant spirit and the cheerful nature of childhood is ever a comforting boon in the distress and helplessness of early life, and soothes the heart in trouble, and brings rest to the mind. So in this case Nora's mind, after an hour of deepest grief and gloom, found quiet and repose, for new hope brightened up her mind with cheering words of promise.

The sun was now descending in the west; the tall pines on the mountain tops and slopes were casting long, dark shadows over the mountain sides; waning day was bringing on the night which would close the saddest and most eventful day of Nora's life.

She climbed upon, a huge granite rock, which seemed to offer her some safety for the night. Standing there, and looking around anxiously, in the purity and innocence of childhood, with the birds singing their plaintive twilight song, and the gentle evening breeze sighing through the forest a sad sort of whispered prayer, she seemed more like one of the happy and blessed ones above than the sad and sorrowing ones of earth.

Feeling her helplessness now in this her time of great need, realizing the grandeur and incomprehensible immensity of the mountains as contrasted with herself, and inspired with a feeling of reverence for Him who created these wondrous hills and mountains, she dropped upon her knees, and seemingly in resignation to the chastening power of the Divine will raised her hands imploringly to heaven, and in prayer, besought God to look down upon her in mercy; to deliver her from the terrors and dangers which surrounded her; prayed to Him to guide and protect her Uncle Drew from misfortune and death, and to direct his footsteps to her side; and that others be mercifully protected from the sorrows, and misfortunes which she that day had suffered. Then she lay down upon the rock, resigning herself to the bitter circumstances which controlled her, and which she could not alter. She soon fell into a quiet slumber. Exhausted nature brought to her weakened frame the refreshing sleep she so much needed.

It should be stated in connection herewith, for the information of those not acquainted with the peculiar atmospheric conditions of the Rocky Mountain region, that the frequency, and the destructive violence of floods of this sort have been much increased since its invasion by civilized man. For the Indian in his wisdom—grudgingly granted him—was a conservator of the mountain forests and of nature in its primitive beauty. But the white man on the contrary with his wanton, wasteful forest fires, with the woodman's and lumberman's axe has almost completely shorn the mountains of their beautiful evergreen forests and many of their shrubs and flowers, thus leaving the rag-

NORA ALONE IN THE MOUNTAINS

ged rocks bare, and grinning as it were, in mockery of this senseless work of destruction.

Seemingly, in chastening retaliation for this, and as if angered at the disturbance of their quiet solitude and repose, the mountains now hurl down their denuded sides and through their gulches, with increased violence and force, the outpour from the heavy water-laden clouds, unrestrained in its flow by neither bush, tree nor shrub, into the gulches below, thus forming in them immense rivers of water which rush down their steep, descending channels with indescribable fury and force, most terrifying to behold.

One of the most horrible of these floods, evidently largely augmented by these causes, occurred on the evening of July 4, 1896, at Morrison, in this state, extending north to Golden.

At this time of the year the mountains are filled with people from the cities who, with their children, are taking relief from the heat in the cool breezes of the mountains. On, and along the banks of Bear Creek, above Morrison, has always been a favourite resort for pleasure seeking outing parties. Upon these unwarned, helpless people in the darkness of midnight, without a moment's notice, came one of these floods, roaring like distant thunder, with a crack of breaking trees, and rumbling rocks. In a moment the flood, a rapidly advancing wall of water, boulders and drift-wood, was upon them, carrying their summer dwellings and tents along, and crushing them like an egg shell. Many people sleeping in their beds were enveloped in its pitiless embrace, its titanic power crushing them down to the earth and burying them beneath its irresistible advance. It would be futile to attempt to describe in detail the horrors and frightful destruction of this terrific flood. Furthermore it would not be pleasing, because the horrors of a disastrous death awakens sympathy and brings sadness and sorrow to the heart.

Suffice it to say that the wall of water, retarded and held upward by timber, driftwood and brush, came rushing down the gulch more than ten feet high, tearing trees out of the earth, carrying away with it houses, barns and bridges, ploughing out great channels for itself and destroying everything in its path. A few escaped, some in a miraculous manner. Little Irene Proctor was lifted into the air by a saving bush and thus held till her cries attracted heroic rescuers. Another saved his life by catching hold of a tree top and climbing to safety. In all twenty-five people lost their lives at Morrison on this occasion, mostly business and professional people from Denver. The two accomplished daughters of J. W. Horner, a Denver attorney, lost their lives in Mt. Vernon gulch, near, but north of Bear Creek. It required the combined labour of one hundred and seventy men and fifty horse teams for many days to repair the roads and bridges destroyed at Morrison by this awful flood.

The next morning the rising sun, shining in Nora's face,

awoke her to a realization of her friendless condition, in a wild and unexplored mountain region. But feeling the pangs of hunger, and inspired by a spirit of determination and heroism, which the necessities of her pitiable condition demanded, with a whispered prayer she firmly resolved to quit forever the sad scenes which surrounded her, and, if possible, find protection and friends. Taking the soiled blanket on her arm, excitedly, she started over the mountains, more in a run than a walk. Whence she knew not. Over tumbled, disordered piles of loose rock, through thickets of underbrush and dense pine forests she went, sometimes walking, sometimes running and panting like a frightened fawn, till from sheer exhaustion she was obliged to proceed more slowly.

Coming into a small opening in the forest, in a deep gulch of the mountains, she was delighted beyond expression, for upon the ground before her she beheld a feast of beautiful red mountain strawberries, of which she eagerly partook, and which gave her increased strength to continue her journey. She travelled up this gulch for many miles, and at last was rewarded by a discovery which made her heart leap with joy. For she found blazed trees, the woodman's mark of a pathway in the forest, and other evidences of white men's work, for the Indians, then also roamed the mountains.

She was assured by these and other evidences that she was really on a trail made by people of her own race.

Increased hope and anxiety lightened her steps, and she hastily followed the course of the blazed line of the winding trail. At last she beheld with delight a miner's rude habitation or cave. It was situated in the mountains, as near as can be now ascertained, in the forest somewhere on Bear Creek above Evergreen, southwest of Bergen Park. It was an excavation in the mountain side, built up with round logs. The roof consisted of small poles covered with pine boughs, which in turn were covered with earth. The back part of the cave was thus no higher than the side of the mountain at that point against which it was built. (This circumstance occasioned a strange incident, to be related hereafter.) The door was peculiar. To explain this queer door, more clearly, it should be stated that in cutting out the logs for the door they were sawed off with a double bevel, the saw track forming the letter V and the cut ends of the door logs were thus in the shape of obtuse wedges. For at that time, locks and hinges, except of wood, were not to be had, for the early pioneer carried nothing with him but the important necessities of life.

This fact somewhat explains the origin of the hospitable and prevalent custom of that day among miners and cattle men of leaving their cabins open to the wanderer and the stranger, for they could not lock them. Earth formed the floor, mud and logs the walls; a small hole in the wall served as a window.

Into this rude habitation Nora cautiously entered and

A FEAST OF MOUNTAIN STRAWBERRIES

found flour, matches, bacon, coffee, sugar, salt and, also pans and other light cooking utensils in use in camp life. She also found a notice scribbled on the wall with charcoal which read: "Eat, but steal not." She inferred from this admonition that the owners of this rude habitation were of a kindly disposition, and that they contemplated returning at some future time for their provisions.

It should be here stated that in sparsely settled portions of the west this generous and humane custom prevails to this day among the cowboys and miners. They leave their cabins open to the "cattlemen" and wandering gold miner, who thus find food and shelter in the absence of the "boss," who may be from home and he perhaps finds food and shelter in the hospitable cabin of a stranger in like manner.

The sad spirit of poor Nora now was made hopeful in the thought that she at some future time perhaps would be rescued from the terrors which surrounded her on all sides. For Indians, bears and mountain lions then existed in abundance in the mountains.

So she wisely concluded to wait for the return of the unknown occupants of the cabin, for she felt instinctively that she could never find her way out of the mysterious and unknown regions of the mountains unaided. She therefore made a fire, and cooked, and ate her first sad and lonely meal. And thus a melancholy life of solitude was begun by her in a wild region, and in a stranger's cabin.

When she had finished her repast, and cleared the table of its queer assortment of dishes, which consisted mostly of tinware, cups, spoons, plates, a case knife, and a steel hunter's knife, she sat down upon a large rock, evidently designed for a seat, and looked around to ascertain the best means to make her enforced home in the cabin endurable. She observed that two round pine logs of suitable lengths placed in the corner of the cabin formed the side, and end of a bunk, the other side and end being formed by the side and end of the cabin. It was filled with dry grass as a substitute for a mattress. There was also a table, but a queer one it was. A sheet, or slab of bark, cut and carefully peeled from a green tree, pressed flat, and dried in the sun, smooth and flat as a board, formed its top. It was three feet wide by four feet long, and was supported by four large rocks. But it flashed upon her mind that she had no change of linen, nor would her well worn dress last her long. She arose from her seat excitedly as she realized this, and walked the room in deep study. She finally concluded that she needed clothing and must have it at all hazards. She knew that if she could secure the dairy can containing her wardrobe from the cavern in the mountain where she had hid it, that she could pass the time in the cabin with tolerable comfort. But it was a fearful and perilous task for her to attempt the trip unguided and alone. But she made up her mind to do so, come what would. For woman's love of dress is to her a meed of praise or the open door, leading down to the lowly walks of shame, dishonour, and death. Therefore, casting all thoughts of danger aside, she started next morning on her perilous journey, taking with her, however, a small lunch. She followed the trail which had guided her to the cabin, back to the foot of a high mountain, where it terminated. For this mountain, now known as Big Chief, adjacent to Bergen Park, was a guide point, because it stands high above the others, and can be easily found, therefore the blazed trees, or trail, began at this mountain and lead to this cabin. From this place Nora succeeded in finding her way, for she recognized many of the mountains which she had previously passed, which aided her very much in arriving at the scene of her great misfortune. She viewed it again with a deeply troubled heart, and made a short search to find what she could; but no additional object was found. So hastily taking hold of the heavy dairy can containing her clothing, she started upon her return journey, sometimes carrying it, sometimes dragging it over the gravelly soil, like a sled, by its handle, till she reached again her cabin door.

The reader can better imagine, than could be described, the sorrow, the dread and anxiety of little Nora during this time. But once during this time did she feel the dangers and terrors of her situation, although at no time did she feel safe. On this occasion she wrapped herself in her blanket and retired for the night, as usual. Stretching herself out on her rude pallet of soft pine twigs, she soon fell into a quiet sleep, but some time during the night she heard a rumbling noise overhead, like heavy footsteps on the weak, trembling roof. This both awoke and alarmed her. Suddenly, with a crash, some huge object came down through the roof and dropped beside her. For a moment she thought it was a rock from the high mountain which had rolled down its side and crashed through the frail roof. But no, it was a living animal of some sort, for its sniff of the air, and its loud, ex-cited breathing filled her heart with fear and trembling. Its warm, strong breath, which beat often heavily into her face, increased her fright, for she thus knew that it was a large animal, perhaps a grizzly bear. Her situation was now one of intense excitement and terror, and scarcely endurable. But with a fortitude, born of self-reliance and determination, she bore up under this excitement until morning, when she saw by the first light of dawning day that the cause of her alarm was an innocent work-ox that had strayed away from its owner, and wandered onto the roof, which was too weak to bear his weight, and he broke through, dropping a distance of but seven feet to the floor below and thus frightening our young heroine out of her wits. It was not a difficult task to drive him out of the cabin. When outside he started off bellowing, in search of his mate, while Nora engaged herself in the work of repairing the damage to her domicile; for having been reared on a farm, she was capable of doing much of the outdoor work of boys or men. She could fish, trap rabbits or grouse with the skill of a hunter, in which she often engaged, and fortunately, while in this solitude, with advantageous results.

The possession of these rude accomplishments, fishing and hunting, were the source of much pleasure to her in her solitude and isolation. By engaging in them she was thus beguiled into a new line of thought, and into a forgetfulness of her condition. Thus was the tedium of time and the weary watching and waiting during many a dull day lightened and lifted from her mind. The pleasing excitement of these pursuits also brightened her mind with the light of joy, like rays of light through a cloud-covered sky. Indeed she became fascinated, and attached to this sort of recreation and pastime. But as she possessed a bright mind of diversified qualities, she was enabled to pursue various other sources of amusement. One of these was efforts of a literary nature, and the composition of short poems, one of which is presented:

Nora's Soliloquy

Oh, solitude, banish the gloom, which disturbs my breast,
And tell me, oh, tell me, why I'm oppressed
With dread, and with fear, and full of alarm,
And why thy grandeur, to me, is void of a charm?

Thy silence is dreary, and hard to endure
While I wander about, and seek for its cure,
In the midst of the forest, along the bright stream,
Where fishes are skipping, so happy they seem.

And the gay, feathered songsters, on perches above
Are sending up music, to God, for his love.
While leaflet, and limb, of the majestic trees,
Fanned by the breeze, make music to please.

And the voice of the stream, as it rushes along,
Yields up its music, and grants me a song,
Though sweet be the songs of bird, brook and tree,
They are sad to my heart—dull music to me.

They fill me with anguish, for in them I see
The cause of their joy, and not any for me.
I shrink from the view, in gloom and vexation,
For I'm but a speck in God's pondrous creation;

And a victim of forces, controlling the world
As seen in flood-waters, or lava of volcanoes hurled.
How, then, can I be merry, while lost, and alone,
Homeless and friendless, and the future unknown?
For watching and waiting is distressing to me;
Oh how I long for its ending—I pray it soon be.

But as all things of this world have a termination, so
Nora's exile was approaching its end. Snow had now
clothed the high mountain peaks in white, though none
had fallen in the narrow gulch where Nora dwelt, but the
keen frost of September had touched the leaves of the
aspen and wild raspberry, and they were falling in showers
to the ground. These signs of approaching winter instead
of diminishing her hope, as one would suppose, rather
increased it, for with the sound reasoning of one of more
mature years, she felt sure that the proprietors of the provisions and cabin would surely return now for their store
of winter supplies, deposited there, perhaps, to lighten the

loads of their pack animals while they travelled over the almost impassable mountains in search of rich gold mines. This view of the matter was correct, for on the 5th day of October of the year 1860, a memorable day to her, she met with an episode and, though not unexpected, it was none the less exciting. She had been out that day hunting and fishing. The fish she caught with a dip net, made of strips of strong willow bark; the rabbits and grouse with snares or loops of the same, set where they resort, into which they ran, and were thus caught. She had that day caught two grouse and was cooking them over a gentle fire, and had stepped outside the door to go for a pail of water, when she heard distinctly these words, while her heart rapidly beat with joy:

"Say, pard, would it not be a joke on us if the mountain rats and gophers have eaten up all our grub."

"No, it would be a greater joke to find it there, for we did not think of the voracious mountain rats when we left, and it is but reasonable to think they have destroyed it."

Nora stood as one in a trance. She heard footsteps approaching, and saw glimpses of dusky figures through the thick pines. As they came nearer she saw that they were two rough-looking white men, in ragged clothing, with lengthy unshaven beards, and long uncut hair. They drove before them two mules laden with blankets, picks, shovels and other articles pertaining to a miner's life.

When they saw her standing there pail in hand, they were more surprised than she. But as they came close to her, a puzzled smile came upon the face of one of them, and he said excitedly:

"Oh, Nora, what brought you here, and are you alone?"

Nora looked upon him with surprise and wonder, and gave him a searching look.

"Sad and in sorrow am I, yes, alas! alone."

"Alone," said Nora, as she broke down under a spasm of grief, realizing the true meaning, to her, of the word, "alone."

And she wept, as women often weep, from the high excitement and emotions of the occasion. For there was much to disturb and harass her mind. She did not know the character of the men, whether honourable or not. She would now have to relinquish her independence, and appeal to them for guardianship and care, and for just and fair treatment, for she was now in their power.

These considerations agitated her much as she looked upon these two strange men with that insecurity which the absence of knowledge yields.

Feeling, however, that friendly regard, and respectful confidence, will win favour, and permitting her mind to reach out to them with trusting hope, she therefore, while they unpacked, and turned their mules out to graze, explained to them her sad situation, told them of her misfortune, of the death of her parents and of the probable death of her Uncle Drew by some wild animal, and closed by asking earnestly:

"Who are you?"

Why, Nora, is it possible that you do not recognize me yet? I am Enoch Allen, whom you met on the plains and a true friend to you now in your time of greatest need, for my sympathy is drawn out to you by the affecting recital of your misfortune and sorrow."

"Oh, will you be a friend to me?" she said imploringly, as she flung her arms around his body in trusting hope. "And will you be a father to me, and take me out of these terrible mountains?"

"Yes, Nora," he said, as sympathetic tears glistened in his eyes, "I will give you a father's care and protection."

They then entered the cabin, and while an exceedingly

pleasant conversation was entered into, and mutual explanations were made Nora, with cheerful face and pleasing smile, and with a skill and grace not to be expected of one of her years, completed the preparations of the meal already begun. As they partook of this pleasant repast of mountain grouse and trout and pancakes, it seemed that never could people be more happy than they then were. In reply to an apology, made by Nora for appropriating his provisions to her own use, Enoch said: "Reproach yourself not, Nora, for you had no choice in the matter, and I would not be human to blame you for what you could not avoid; and besides I think you deserve more praise than blame, for your presence in the cabin has doubtless protected the provisions from the depredations of rats and gophers Having been favoured by fortune in my search for gold, being now the possessor of one of the best mines in Russel Gulch, near Central City, and being possessed of plenty, I will 'whack up' with you, as miners say, and furnish you with the necessary means to educate yourself at one of the best academies in St. Louis, and will see you safely out of this lonely place, provided, however, that you will accept my proposition with the generous untrammelled freedom with which it is made, and that you will in no wise feel humiliated by its acceptance, nor be grieved by becoming a dependent upon my benefactions, and a debtor in a sum which you are now powerless to pay."

"Oh, Enoch," she replied, "friend that you now prove yourself to be to me, speak not thus, for your language fills my mind with contending thoughts and emotions, which my poor words have not the power to clearly express. Besides you know that I am lost and forlorn, bound to this spot, for I know not the way out. I am at your mercy, for good or for ill, and therefore can not refuse your offer, whatever it be, or however disagreeable to me."

NORA RETURNING FROM THE BROOK

"Nora, the fine impulses of your nature," said Enoch Allen, "awaken thoughts in your mind which should lie dormant. They fill your troubled heart with entanglements and difficulties which may never arise, and should not be considered at this melancholy time, therefore to persuade you, if possible, to its acceptance, I will now withdraw all its conditions, and will make it again, pure and simple, and will grant to time and the nobility of your nature to wear away the difficulties which disturb your mind. For what I offer to do for you is but a simple act of Christian equity, in line with the golden rule, which means assistance to those in distress, as assistance should be given us if in like need. Assistance, if given at all, should surely come from abundance and not from poverty's purse. I therefore feel that it is surely due from me to you, notwithstanding the scruples you have in this matter, to make you this offer. For in accordance with these views I owe you a debt in Christian equity, and after its payment we but stand as equals under the moral law, each to each. Besides, viewing this matter in another way, we have, through the providence of God, or by the fateful circumstances that control the destinies of men for weal or for woe, been brought to, and placed in, the most striking circumstances with relation to each other. You, cast down into the depths of inexpressible misery and despair by the loss of your parents, and all else that was dear to you, and that made life worth living, while I, with no great effort of my own, but rather by the benevolence of good luck, have been made happy beyond expression by the discovery of a gold mine of inestimable wealth. I think, therefore, as we both have started out together in pursuit of the same object, and as we have been companions in the hardships, dangers and discomforts of travel on the plains, and though you have been lost and forlorn on the way, you still should rightfully out of our mutually acquired wealth, receive salvage, which is the reward due each member composing a company who performed an undertaking full of danger. Under the maritime laws of both England and the United States, salvage is due each member of a party in an adventure, not for any distinct performance of a member of the party, but for the successful performance of the whole. In accordance with this well accepted law, you, Nora, are entitled to a share of my good luck."

Nora, in response, said:

"Enoch, kind sir, I cannot fully comprehend the fine sense of right which you maintain should prevail among mankind, nor do I feel competent to give a logical answer to these sublime and intricate questions of moral law. I therefore prefer to meditate seriously on them in silence, and I can only say you are too kind. I can never repay you, nor can I find words that will tell you how grateful I am for your interest in me."

"I seek not gratitude, nor words of thanks," said Enoch, "but rather the approval of my head and heart; and therefore freely give to others a part of what has been bestowed on me by the wise Dispenser of this world's blessings."

It was arranged, therefore, that his partner or "pard," as he termed him, should transport the provisions to the mine, while Enoch would visit his relatives and friends near St. Louis during the winter, and return in the spring to continue his work in the mines. He would thus be enabled to conduct Nora safely out of danger and place her in school, as he had so generously proffered to do. Next morning the two mules were loaded with their packs, one for Denver, already a little village, the other for the mines of North Clear Creek in Russel Gulch.

Enoch seated Nora on the pack, while he walked, driving the well-laden animal along, as is the custom of miners. At Denver he and Nora took the stage for Omaha, where they boarded the cars for St. Louis, where Nora was to enter St. Mary's Academy, under the watchful and motherly care of the Sisters of that institution.

As Nora was now to receive her education in a Catholic sisterhood, and as she may be affected more or less by its environment, and as these educational institutions are now receiving constantly increasing patronage, many prominent Protestants select them as the most fitting institutions for the education of their daughters, it is pertinent to know something of the inner life and rules governing them. They are organized communities of women, under systematic laws regulating their government, designed to perform religious duties, or do work of charity or benevolence.

Each takes a solemn vow, considered as sacred as an oath, when admitted to the community, to do special religious work, thus the Sisters of Charity are pledged to engage in the vast work which their name implies. The Sisters of the Good Shepherd are pledged to be shepherds in fact, to care for the lambs, the girls, that they go not astray, and keep and guide them in the path of virtue and away from sin. The Little Sisters of the Poor furnish a home for the aged and helpless poor, while others are pledged to perform educational work, imparting religious knowledge to the young, inculcating into their minds honour and reverence to God, and disciplining their young minds in manners and morals.

To enable them to carry out these benevolent purposes, unrestrained and untrammelled, they are pledged solemnly to celibacy, whereby they may devote their care to this work, rather than to a husband and family.

The pledge of celibacy carries with it many subsidiary requirements. The celibate is admonished to walk the streets with modest, downcast eyes, not to talk with men, only as necessity requires, nor engage in jocular nor frivolous talk. These observances followed for years as near as weak human nature can yield to them, establishes a modest and attractive manner in the Catholic Sisters always discernible. For modest and dignified grace is a crown and glory in lovely women far surpassing in value gold or a jewelled crown. No wonder then, that Martin Luther, in the grossness of sin, cast away his priestly robes, and heedless of his sacred vow, married a nun and originated a religion, not named after any divine person, but named after himself, and which finally unscrupulous kings found in it pretended excuse for strife and war, and an apparent cause for the appropriation of the church property by an act of sequestration, a polite name for theft.

Therefore, Nora, surrounded by the modesty and Christian grace of the sisters, could not but be influenced, and her manners modified and shaped, by their refined Christian deportment. It will be shown further on how her dignity and refined manners affected Enoch Allen.

It is not necessary to enter into any detailed account of Nora's life while in the academy, but it must be said of her that she made rapid progress in her studies, due to diligent application and perseverance. She felt that she should conscientiously use what was bestowed upon her for a special purpose, and that to do otherwise would be a wrong to her benefactor. Thus inspired by a sense of duty, and being possessed of a bright intellect, she became one of the brightest students at the school.

Before Enoch Allen returned to Colorado in the spring he paid a visit to Nora. Again she scarcely recognized him, for the barber and clothier had so wonderfully changed his personal appearance that he seemed no longer the same. He was both genteel and well mannered, having a mind disciplined to adapt itself to any condition of life. He again assured Nora that he would fulfil his promise and furnish her the means to acquire an education, and begged her to quiet her modest reluctance in accepting so much from him.

"It is but a trifle," he said, "as compared with the vast sum realized from my mine, and I will never miss so small a sum."

As his mine proved, year after year, to be one of the most productive in Russel Gulch, the yearly remittances for Nora's tuition and expenses were, in fact, as he had said, a trifle to him. He was now a wealthy man, and made occasional visits to his relatives at St. Louis, and on these occasions never failed to call on Nora. It was but natural that a feeling of strong friendship should attract them one to the other, for friendship and love spring not from senseless impulse or passion, but from the mutual appreciation of the good qualities and character of each other.

Nora was now twenty years old, when woman is in the prime of her beauty, in form and face divine, and is then ever a source of pleasure to behold.

Days, months and years had passed, till now Nora had entered upon her fourth and last year at school, and excepting the necessary "shopping" and a few picnic excursions, Nora had never been out of school during all this time. She, therefore, longed for the open fields, the hills and valleys, the wild flowers and sweet song birds of country life. These pleasant scenes of her childhood were dear to her, and she longed to enjoy them again. An opportunity to do so was now unexpectedly granted

her. through the generosity and kindness of two of her old school mates, who offered her' the hospitality of their home and a free passage thereto. This she thankfully accepted and communicated her intentions to Enoch Allen in Colorado. These two young ladies and Nora were great friends during the long years of their school life. Indeed, from their very first acquaintance they were attracted to each other by some influential power or affinity. They became strong and steadfast friends, advised with each other on the trivial vexations and troubles of schoolgirl life. They never seemed more happy than when together, engaged in the animated and innocent prattle which schoolgirls so much delight in. They all entered school at the same time. They were sisters, and though possessing the family name of Norton, were as different from Nora Norton as day is from night. Their complexions were very dark, cheek bones high, eyes dark as a crow's wing, and hair as dark and straight as an Indians; indeed it was whispered among their schoolmates that they were half breeds, but, as two Mexican pupils were as dark as they, with similar cast of features, little was said or thought of the matter. The name of the elder one was Minnie, and the younger one was Annie. Their home was at Fort Laramie, in Wyoming Territory, and because of that circumstance they were supposed to be daughters of an army officer on duty there. They were esteemed by their classmates, being courteous and pleasant to all, and possessing abundant means to meet every need. Indeed they had been so liberally supplied with money that they were amply able to purchase the railroad and stage tickets for themselves and Nora to their home at Fort Laramie, Wyoming Territory.

Fort Laramie, on a tributary of the Platte of that name, was at that time a small frontier post of considerable importance, where several companies of soldiers were stationed to keep the Ute and Cheyenne Indians under control. The officers dwelt in neat frame houses, the soldiers had good quarters, and all lived a life of leisure and pleasure, "Uncle Sam" paying the bills. The sutler, the merchant of the post, besides furnishing the post with tobacco, liquors and other goods at a vast profit, also supplied the Indians with sugar, bacon, crackers, powder, lead, etc., at extortionate prices, often trading a pound of sugar for a tanned buckskin worth a dollar, or 75 cents worth of ammunition for a dressed buffalo robe, worth $5. Thus do Indians, under the care of the agents and officers of the government, see and feel the nobility of civilization, a double-edged sword of injustice which robs them of their means of existence and fills them with misery and despair. And thus it was that the sutler, appointed by the government, and, therefore, secure from any competition, was enabled in a short time to become immensely wealthy. He resided in one of the most beautiful houses of the Fort, and even at that time it had all the style of an eastern mansion. But there is a custom in connection with his life, as well as that of nearly all Indian traders, which must not be omitted in this narration.

They, as a rule, are married to squaws, and thus they are, in a measure, adopted into the tribe, and are considered by the Indians as friends to be trusted. It should also be stated that these white men, or "squaw men," thus connected by marriage feel more safe among the Indians. It is said that a white man's Life among the Indians would not be safe unless he thus connected himself with the tribe. A strange feature of such a marriage is that the would-be bridegroom usually buys his wife for so much merchandise, or a pony. The terms and conditions of the trade are easy. The giving away of the bride and the marriage consist of a feast and a dance of joy—all as simple and rude as a child's play at school.

Hence the sutler at Fort Laramie had likewise long since married a squaw, and had two well-grown half breed daughters whom he had himself taught to read in early life; but, desiring to give them the advantage of a thorough education, now that he was wealthy, he planned to send them to some eastern seminary.

It is worthy of note, before proceeding further, to describe the wonderful change wrought upon the squaw-wife by her marriage to a white man, that instead of the slovenly, unclean condition of her maidenhood, she becomes a comparatively clean and orderly housekeeper. Unlike many women of a higher civilization who esteem their haughty independence so highly that it becomes rank injustice, the squaw-wife has a watchful care, and kindly regard for the pleasure and comfort of her husband. This is mainly due to the family rule in Indian strict life obedience and respect for parental authority; not resistance, but assent to it: not opposition, but compliance with it. This rule, perhaps too strenuous in savage life, is too lax in civilized life.

As many of the army officers' wives and families had now come to reside at the Fort, and as his wealth and position drew around him refined people, and his squaw-wife could never assimilate nor associate with them with any degree of pleasure to either, she seemed to him to be in the way. He therefore planned and put into execution what others before him had done—the most melancholy act of this anomalous marriage. He told his wife, for he had learned to speak the Indian language, that she must return to her tribe; that she could no longer dwell under his roof; that he would send their daughters away to school, and that she, too, must go.

Then, moved by strong and tender love for her children, she ran in frantic grief to the lawn, where they were at play. Seizing the elder one, in endearing tones she cried: "O, Minetah!" which was her Indian name, and wept over her and in a similar manner grieved over Annetah, her younger child.

Regardless of her remonstrance and tears, and unmoved by her pitiful appeals for justice and the right to abide with and enjoy the comforting companionship of her children, the next day he placed her on a pony, with provisions and blankets, and started her off alone, many miles, to seek the camp of her tribe. Though untutored as she was she felt the great wrong to herself of leaving all behind her. She wept all the way, and her loud sobs and wail of sorrow were heard when she was a long distance off. Her children were also in the deepest grief at the loss of their mother. The whole proceeding was extremely sad. But the father's will is the law of the family in Indian as well as in civilized life, whether right or wrong, but it is nevertheless often unjust.

As a soldier had been detailed to the sutler as cook and housekeeper by the commanding officer of the post, the absence of their mother did not affect their personal comfort, but it took from them a mother's sympathy, society and companionship.

Before their departure for school, behold one evening their mother returned on the same pony, after an absence of but two weeks. With tears and entreaties she humbly plead to live and die near her children, for her tribe now treated her with scorn and indifference. Her husband yielded in a measure to her entreaties, for he was not at heart a bad man, but was rather the creature of circumstances. It was agreed that she should live alone in a tent near his house, the abode of her children, and that he would supply all her wants, which were few. This delighted her children, for they could thus call in to see their mother ever day. And it should be said that their squaw-mother really enjoyed these periodical visits more than her daughters, for what mother's heart is not full of joy when her children are playfully romping around her? Time did not hang heavily upon her, because the visits of her children were sunshine to her heart. Now, left to herself in her abode she dropped back to many of the ways of savagery. She preferred a seat upon an open robe to a chair, bed of blankets to a mattress, and her hair loose, hanging down, than done up. As a whole her life was now comparatively happy. To pass the time away, like her more cultured sisters, she engaged in fancy work, making beaded slippers, belts and baskets, which she lovingly bestowed upon Minnie, Annie and her husband.

Soon after this episode the girls were placed on an eastbound stage coach, in care of a returning officer, and taken to an eastern school.

They made annual returns in vacation to see their father and mother. They had their father's consent to invite a schoolmate to visit and remain with them during vacation, but never found one at liberty or willing to undertake so distant, or so arduous a trip. But now they wrote to their father that after graduating they would bring with them to their far western home a dear friend and schoolmate, friendless and alone in the world, to make a long visit with them. They had communicated to their father the date of their departure and he was, therefore, at the overland stage station when they arrived. His two daughters were first on the landing, and after greeting their father, they introduced him, saying: "Father, Miss Nora Norton." He looked upon her in a sort of bewildered surprise, not recognizing her, however, as any one he had previously seen, he received her with a smile rather than with words. But Nora, with that keen discernment and quick decision common to woman-kind, gave him an earnest, searching look, and recognizing him as her uncle Drew, she raised her hands excitedly in the air as the blood rushed to her head and heart from the impulse of the shock, then she ran to him with open arms saying: "Oh, Uncle Drew, do you not know Nora, your niece?" and fell into his arms in a swoon.

And thus Nora and her uncle met so unexpectedly after each had mourned the other as dead.

When Nora regained consciousness a series of explanations were entered into by both, by which each was made acquainted with the sad events in the life of the other, after they had separated so unexpectedly in the gulch in the mountains. Drew told Nora of his fight with the bear; how he lay under a tree all night, and next morning, after eating some of the meat of the bear he had killed, how he had felt increased strength, and after providing himself with some meat for the trip, started to overtake his brother and family, but on entering the gulch where he had left them the day before and seeing its torn-up condition, and finding his brother's hat and remnants of his wagon, and the horse previously mentioned, and after giving the gulch a thorough search for a long distance along its channel, and finding no traces of his brother and family, and being well acquainted with the destructive power of a cloud burst, he concluded that all his brother's family had been drowned, and he, therefore, made his way back to the camp an Cherry Creek, where he took the overland stage for his home at Fort Laramie.

He gave as a reason for withholding a knowledge of his business and family relations from his brother and his family that he feared a rebuke from his brother, who knew nothing of the necessity of his marrying a squaw, and he would, therefore, doubtless condemn him for it.

Nora told her Uncle Drew the long, sad story of her parents' terrible death and of her lost and sad condition in the lonely cabin; of her rescue, and of the generosity of her benefactor. Her uncle was much affected, and said, excitedly:

"I will bestow upon him a small fortune for those inestimable acts of benevolence to you."

"His proud and noble spirit could never be made to yield to an acceptance of a reward for what he finds a pleasure and delight in doing," replied Nora. "Besides, uncle, he is 'the architect of his own fortune,' having made it in the gold mines of Colorado."

"He is a nobleman, truly," said her uncle, "and I would be too glad to meet him and thank him personally, but you have not made known to me his name."

"You have met him once or twice at our camp fire on the plains. His name is Enoch Allen."

"Ah, yes; I remember him. Write to him, Nora, and convey to him my desire to see him, and the pleasure it would afford me for him to visit us."

"It is already arranged, uncle," she said. He will soon be here; but he does not know who you are—nor did I expect so strange a surprise."

"Well," said her uncle, "he will receive a hearty welcome when he comes and be an honoured member of our household, esteemed for his great kindness to you. And Nora, you shall ever have a permanent home with us now."

Nora earnestly thanked him for this evidence of his affection for her. She now felt at home in her uncle's house, and as Minnie and Annie were dear to her before, they seemed more dear to her, now that she knew they were her cousins. She often went into the tent to see their mother, who exhibited much affection for them, and they on these occasions seemed very fond of her.

Their mother addressed them as Minetah and Annetah, which they modified into Minnie and Annie when they entered the academy.

A fortnight after Nora's arrival at the fort, Enoch Allen arrived, which was the occasion again of rejoicing and congratulations. Nora, now so unexpectedly having found a home among loved ones, was as happy as mortal could well be. Her heart, at one time weighed down by heavy sorrow, made life seem to her scarcely worth the living, but now, on the contrary, in the midst of the beauty around her, with loving friends as cheerful companions, and with a heart full of joy, she rejoiced that life was a blessing of such inexpressible worth. She now longed to see Enoch, to tell him of her great joy and rehearse to him some of the incidents connected with her dreary, isolated life in the cabin, which, for want of time, and a suitable opportunity at the convent, she had never told him.

As no definite day had been fixed upon for the arrival of Enoch Allen, Nora and her uncle took occasional walks to the station at "coach time," in the hope of meeting him, which they did on an incoming coach a fortnight after Nora's arrival at her uncle's. Nora scarcely recognized him in his neat-fitting suit of black, covering his robust and shapely form. As he alighted from the coach, she eagerly approached him, and with a refined manner and dignity she gracefully extended to him her welcoming hand, and as he took it in his, in tones well spoken, and seemingly as sweet to him as the sounds of a sweet song bird, she said:

"Enoch Allen, my most esteemed friend, I grasp your hand with a feeling of gratitude and respect, for I have been an undeserving recipient of your substantial generosity, and therefore it delights me highly to meet you, and express to you my gratitude."

Looking upon her with admiration and delight, he replied: "Nora, the melody of your voice, the readiness with which you speak, and the beauty of your language, please and charm me, which is ample reward to me for the little I have done for you, for by your studious industry at the academy, my paltry and voiceless gold has adorned you with an eloquence and beauty of speech more sweet than music itself, therefore let your mind repose in peace: for it has benefited you and done me no harm, for I have an abundance of money—beyond my needs."

Nora, in the excitement of her interview with Enoch, and during this interesting colloquy with him, had overlooked or forgotten her uncle, who stood near by listening, and waiting. Looking around, she saw him, whereupon she informally introduced Enoch. Her uncle took him cordially by the hand, and said:

"It is a pleasure to me to meet you—you who have been so generous a benefactor to my most unfortunate niece. I appreciate your kindness, and hope to reward you, or reciprocate the favour, at some future time."

"I would degrade myself in my own conscious knowledge of my duty, did I not respond to the cry of distress and reach out a helping hand to the unfortunate, and helpless to aid them to arise," modestly replied Enoch. "The beasts of the field and the birds of the air fly to their companions in distress, to give battle and protect them in their helpless need. I would have been less than one of these had I not, out of my vast, inflowing abundance, given assistance to your worthy niece."

Nora, hearing these tender and noble words come from the lips of Enoch, was moved by emotions of gratitude, and her eyes filled with tears, and she wept as women often weep, from uncontrollable excitement. The scene was an affecting one as they stood together, Nora in the acme of the superlative beauty of early womanhood, adorned by educational accomplishments, and Enoch Allen, in the grandeur of robust manhood, was an interesting sight to behold.

"Enoch, your words are wisely spoken, and manifest a generous disposition and a nobility of character which awakens my admiration, and wins my love and respect." said her uncle.

The conversation was of too exciting a nature for Nora to enjoy or endure, so she remarked, before Enoch had time to reply: "Let us go to the house," which they all did.

Entering the parlour, an artistically and elaborately furnished room. Nora's uncle pointing to a luxuriant easy chair, while she gracefully relieved him of his hat, offered an apology for temporary absence on the plea of personal business, and left Enoch and Nora together alone, as it may be supposed, to their great satisfaction. It is needless to say that a woman is always the first to break an oppressive silence, when alone with the man she admires and respects. So it was in this case. Nora, with the fertility of a trained mind, gracefully broke the silence and charmed the ears of Enoch by the eloquent and captivating manner of her recital of the exciting incidents of her life. As she related incident after incident in detail of her striking adventures, of the stringency of her environment, and how her ingenuity enabled her to overcome them, Enoch, an attentive and interested listener, seemed to be entranced by the charm of her manner. The ready flow of her well-chosen words falling from her lips, the melody of her well-modulated voice, and the charming modesty resting in her eyes and on her brow, the crown of glory over all, won Enoch's regard and he had to admit to himself that Nora possessed a mind of marvellous power. His admiration of her intellectual qualities gained his favour, and thus was dullness and inattention aroused into pleasing action. Then the little midget, love, found easy access, and a hiding place within the inner recesses of his heart. Her personal charms, and brilliant accomplishments, spread their captivating influence around him. He became an easy victim to its potent power, and he felt himself drawn with tenderness toward Nora. His heart was inspired with strong love for her. But to explain this condition of his heart to her was a serious matter to him, for she had always been more a child to him than an equal, to whom he might talk of love, and he had always seemed more like a father to her. Nevertheless, he formed a resolution to make known to her his affection and love for her, which had irresistibly found its way into his mind and heart. He awaited a favourable opportunity with pleasurable suspense. As they frequently strolled out together for a walk, or to view the soldiers on parade, or to see them go through the manual of arms, the opportunity was not long in presenting itself.

One day, while sitting on a long summer seat in the shade of a large tree, viewing the soldiers on dress parade, going through the beautiful changes of the march, Enoch Allen remarked to Nora:

"That is a pleasing sight to behold."

"I aver it is, and it shows the grand results of educational training," answered Nora.

"Truly said," replied Enoch. "But beauty is not alone a source of joy. I venture to say that these soldiers are neither content nor happy."

"They appear to be, but appearances are often deceiving," said Nora. "As their daily service is well understood, they are free from care, responsibility, and the vexation of a business life, and should therefore be extremely happy."

"Ah! Nora! These are insufficient to satisfy the requirements of the active, intelligent mind of man. It requires pleasing employment to cheer and make it happy, for idleness is nothing. It is the absence of everything."

"Enoch, you speak so seriously, so solemnly, that I suppose you are gloomy today."

"Nora, your surmises are not far wrong, for my mind is filled with a sort of trouble."

"Enoch Allen, friend of mine that you are, tell me what troubles you, that I may give you aid and comfort. I thought that you possessed everything that makes the heart of man happy."

"No, dear Nora—allow me so to call you—there is one thing more I desire, to make me completely happy—it is your own dear self. I want your rich, pure love. I want you to be my own sweet wife."

As he spoke these words, apparently so unexpected to her, she fell over in a faint against his shoulder, or seemingly so, possibly to hide the excitement of her overpowering joy. This so surprised and excited him, he quickly arose, laid her down in a restful position, with his soft felt hat under her head as a substitute for a pillow, but soon reaction set in, and returning consciousness was visible, and as she opened her eyes a gentle, quiet smile came over her beautiful face as sweet as that of a babe, awakening from slumber.

"Oh! dear Nora! dear Nora!" he said, as he raised her to an upright position, "Pardon me for my haste and rudeness."

She laughed merrily, but gently, and said: "Perhaps you are not aware that young ladies intuitively have more discernment than the average man gives them credit for. I was hoping, half expecting, a climax of this sort, but notwithstanding this, my great delight and uncontrollable joy overwhelmed me, and I was made helpless, and in your care for a time at least, and now, dear Enoch, yours for years to come, while life does last," and Enoch took her approvingly by the hand, and sat down by her side. And now we will leave them in the midst of their supreme joy.

[It should be here stated that, in the manner and style of the customary novel or story of the present day, the love scene is made a jumble of nonsense, of cooing and kissing, of petting, fondling and pleading, which is a needless display of the low, animal grossness of our vulgar nature, for could the average love-making scenes immediately preceding marriage be photographed, and the whole reproduced together on a screen as a "living picture," it would be a startling sight, and one which few would wish to look upon ten years after marriage. This sort of thing should have no attraction for minds of noble qualities and intellectual greatness. But it prevails nevertheless. Marriage is not a mere union of bodies. It is more. It is a union of the higher and nobler qualities of man and woman, the union of a similitude of minds, a union of approving intellects, of genial, longing souls for each other, as exemplified in this true story of Enoch and Nora, who required better evidence of their love for each other than the fallacious, animal-like kiss as simulated in the caressing tongue stroke of the cow and dog, or in the fondling stroke of the bill of birds of land and air. Their noble souls sought the higher and greater joys of intellectual life, which they found in each other. Each found in the mind of the other qualities to admire, not to question or "nag." The emanation of their intellects was always a source of joy to the other, for though differing materially from each other, they were in harmonious accord, as the string of a harp or violin is with its mate. A union of this sort is full of wisdom and joy, more of heaven than of sordid earth. It is a union of two kindred souls reaching out to each in a rebuking frown upon the "nagging" disturber of the peace and quiet of married life.]

The nature and occurrences of the memorable episode of Enoch and Nora on the summer seat under the tree in which their love was plighted to each other, was for some time not known to anyone except themselves. They named the day, however, of their marriage, which was destined to be one of the happiest days of their eventful lives, which they coyly endeavoured not to make known. But the news was too interesting to be kept a secret. Nora and Enoch were now always together, usually in the society of Minnie and Annie. Their uncle, being occupied more or less with his business, had not much time to devote to the numerous social functions of the fort.

Her uncle was delighted with this turn of affairs.

A marriage at a fort on the plains at that time was an episode of very rare occurrence, and caused a stir and an excited interest among the officers' wives and other female attaches.

Uncle Drew had much to do with the conduct and arrangements of the marriage ceremonial. As he had much influence with the commanding officer, his solicitation and wishes respecting the wedding ceremonial were graciously granted. The spacious armoury of the fort was beautifully decorated for the occasion. All needful regulations were provided by Nora's uncle. The line of march from the Norton residence across the lawn was as follows:

In first advance—Chaplain Captain Eastlight, Enoch Allen, Nora Norton, Minnie Norton and Andrew Norton.

Second advance—Guard of honour, consisting of a detachment of fifty United States soldiers, in full dress, in ten lines, five abreast. Third advance—Full military band playing the wedding march. Fourth advance—Invited guests, consisting of commissioned officers of the Fort, the Indian agent and Chief Big Smoke, an Indian interpreter.

Entering the armoury each advance took its place, previously designated, the guard of honour in a decorative manner around the wall, while the others found seats in the body of the hall, the bridal party taking a place well up in front near the chancel.

The chaplain of the fort united them in marriage, her Uncle Drew giving her away with tears of joy in his eyes, for he felt that a man possessing so many good qualities deserved a worthy wife. A large number of friends were present at the ceremony, and their hearty wishes for the future happiness of the newly-wedded pair were an index of the delight and pleasure they felt on the occasion.

On their wedding tour Enoch and his bride visited his relatives at St. Louis, after which they located in Denver and invested the greater portion of his vast wealth in stocks and bonds. He thus lives a life of leisure and quiet content. His splendid residence on one of the fashionable streets, with its beautiful lawn and ornamental shrubbery, is often pointed out to strangers as "the residence of one of the richest men in the city."

Minnie was married to Captain Eastlight. who is stationed in Arizona. Annie married a young merchant and resides in Rochester, N.Y. Their mother died in her tent before the marriage of either of her daughters, having had the best of care and attention in her last illness. Andrew Norton, now an old man, resides with his son-in-law in Rochester, N.Y.

Minta Abel!
The Cow-Herder Girl

It is a pleasing study to contemplate the life history of the distinguished citizens which are found in any community. In whatever capacity they excel, whether in business success, intellectual acquirement, or the possession of great wealth, we long to know the hidden pathway which led them to attain their prominence. While their accomplishments are a wonder, we long to penetrate and possess the secret of their success.

Therefore the struggles and incidents which the great ones of the world have passed through in their upward advancement are highly interesting, and we listen eagerly to their recital. But why the stepping stone to prosperity should often be the most adverse and discouraging, is as inexplicable as that one's eyes should be black, another's blue, or that one child should be born in the midst of the comforts of wealth, while another equally attractive is born in the abode of poverty and suffers from want, hunger, and cold, through all the days of its childhood, or that one should have kind and loving parents, the other one cross and cruel ones. That these various conditions of childhood may or may not seriously affect and somewhat shape the course of life is a question which has engaged the earnest consideration and investigation of the philanthropic minds of men.

Whether any of these conditions or the longings of a bright mind shaped Minta Abel's way in life to triumph over all her misfortunes is left for the reader to judge when he reads her wonderful life story.

Poor Minta was too young, too innocent, to give cause, or do any wrong for which she should be made to suffer, or deserve to be depressed by cruelty and abuse. Yet these were not a shield to her and did not protect her heart from the inflow of sorrow or the desolation of deprivation.

It seemed sad, indeed, when in the providence of God her father was taken from her by death, when she was but a child three years old, thus depriving her of his paternal companionship and care. But it was cruelty, and a misfortune to Minta when, in less than two years after her father's death, her mother married again, and she was compelled to yield obedience and respect to a man who had been a stranger to her till the day he married her mother.

If Minta had had any choice in this matter she would never have chosen Ezra McBride to be her stepfather, for he was repulsive to her the first time she saw him. His gruff, harsh manner and speech grated on the fine feelings of her nature, and she shrank from him as from one she feared.

Ezra McBride had lived too long the careless life of a bachelor, void of business worry and responsibility and was of too gross a nature to bear with patience the whims or wants of childhood, or find any pleasure in their innocent prattle or play. He never spoke in tender tones, nor in the soothing voice so endearing to the pure angel spirit of early childhood. He never addressed Minta but to rebuke, direct or command her in some trivial matter.

The home joys and sunshine of Minta's youth were thus covered by the dark shadow of her stepfather's sordid nature.

He was in no way prepossessing. His features were dark and forbidding, coarse and angular. He had lost one of his front teeth in a fight over a glass of ale, it was said, which added to the peculiarity of his looks. When he spoke in animated, or excited tones, his words came out through the vacant space of his absent tooth, causing a snake-like hissing or whistling sound.

It is one of the inexplicable mysteries of social life to see men and women of the most strange contrasts imaginable joined together in marriage. A union of this sort was the marriage of Ezra McBride and Sarah Abel, the good look-ing young widow. It was accordingly the wonder and the talk of the neighbourhood for many months.

She had a good ranch in scarcely a day's ride from Den-ver, well stocked with cattle, which yielded her a good liv-ing, and it went without saying that Ezra McBride married her more for the love of her home than for her personal attractions.

Be that as it may, the inference was a reasonable one, for he had nothing to add to her small store of wealth. His disregard of, and his harsh manner toward, Minta did not soften with the growing charms of her increasing age, but, on the contrary, he maintained toward her a sort of stern severity and demureness repugnant to her joyous nature.

Minta was now six years old and a child of remarka-ble beauty and intelligence. Her love of knowledge was so strong that she never seemed so happy as when her mother told her over the names of the letters of the alphabet, or when she taught her how to spell small words. Thus Minta almost persuaded her mother by her anxiety and inquiring look to teach her to read, which was an easy task, for she followed her mother from kitchen to cellar with finger on a word to be told its meaning or its pronunciation. Thus she became a good reader at a very early age. Seldom do children manifest so much desire to learn as she did. Books were her joy and reading her delight. She borrowed from neighbours far and near to fill this want. But, like many others who have sought to fill their minds with the gems of knowledge and wisdom,, she did not find the way to do so smooth nor easy, for books were limited, and her neighbours were miles and miles apart in the cattle growing region where she dwelt, and, besides, at her early age, she was, by the exacting nature of her father, obliged to do many outdoor errands. The old "cow pony," a trained and gentle animal, was often saddled for her, and she was compelled to herd and gather in the cows and assist in the milking. And, by gradually increasing her duty, both in doors and out, she became a drudge for both her father and her mother. It was Minta here, Minta there, Minta out and Minta in. From early morning till late at night she was on the go. Having a generous disposition and a kind heart, she was animated by a desire to please, and thought but little of these hardships, but, as time wore on, she was made sadly aware that she could not please her unreasonable and ill-natured father. Her conversation he treated with contempt; her work he unkindly criticised and depreciated and her intelligence he underrated, and called her a silly child, or a fool. And now, to increase her weight of misery, she perceived that her mother extended to her less sympathy than formerly. She thought in her childish heart that her mother had all she could do to care for her little half-sister. Nana, and therefore she could not now give her so much attention, while the fact was that her husband's perverse nature found a hideous pleasure in prejudicing her mother against Minta.

Poor Minta, now cut off from that sympathy and affectionate regard which fill the sweet days of childhood with joyous delight, was cast into gloom. Sadness filled her heart, and now, though but ten years old, she began to think and plan for herself. She therefore determined that she would prove to her father and mother, and others as well, that she had been greatly wronged, and was not weak minded, but would in time fill an honoured place among the educated and intelligent ones of the world. This determination absorbed all the other thoughts of her mind, and she thus became apparently morose, but, in fact, she was intent on working out in a spirit of gloomy hopefulness some plan by which she could accomplish her noble purpose. She was, therefore, serious and reflective during this time, as one oppressed. For most of her time was occupied in herding the cows on the prairies, often five or more miles from her home. She naturally thus became a skilful rider, could ride a horse bareback sideways or otherwise, with a wondrous grace and security. And, as she thus did a "cowboy's" work, she was named "the cowboy-girl" by those who met her on these occasions.

At the beginning of her regular labour as a "cowboy" she met with a most melancholy accident.

She had brought home the cows, and climbing to the top of a stack of hay to get feed for her pony, a wind storm caused her to lose her footing, and she was hurled to the ground, breaking her jaw bone near the joint—which confined her to her bed for several weeks.

Her father, with his characteristic want of sympathy for her, was enraged, for he knew well he would now be obliged to herd the cows himself, for a while at least, and therefore he said to Minta in angry tones as she lay in her bed:

"You ought a had more sense than go on the stack when the wind blowed," hissing the words through the vacant space of his absent tooth. Now, had Minta failed to feed her pony for this cause, he would with his accustomed perversity have said, as he had often before: "No danger of wind a hurtin' you; it never hurts good-for-nothin' folks."

Minta, comprehending this, and knowing his evil nature, and feeling the injustice she was made to bear, said, submissively, while tears filled her eyes:

"Father, I thought that you wanted me to feed the pony."

"Yas, I did." said her father, "but no use in bein' awkard and fallin' off a stak'."

Her mother, now moved with compassion for her child in her misfortune and weakness, said: "Ezra, you are unreasonable in expecting so much from Minta. When she does her work well for one of her age you find fault with her because she does not do it with the skill and nicety of one of more mature years. When she does not do it through forgetfulness, of which you yourself are guilty, or for want of time, you call her lazy and good-for-nothing."

Feeling that there was some truth in what she said, he replied: "Wal. she wurrys me, and I know I hev caus to cumplane."

Mrs. McBride replied: "No doubt you think so, but the 'cause' you mention is an imagined one, existing only in your own mind and due to your exactions and your unreasonable requirements of a child."

"Wal, I know what is best for her, better than you," he replied, hissing the words through the vacant space of his tooth.

"Then, if you know what is best for her, you will get a surgeon and have her jaw set," she said quietly, for she desired to bring this exciting conversation to a close.

"I'll call Dr. Links. He's good e-nuff and it 'ill not cost us so much," said Ezra McBride, feeling a little questionable consolation in the thought that Dr. Links, a quack, and therefore a cheap doctor, would charge less than an experienced and skilful one.

To this, strange as it may seem, Mrs. McBride assented, and the result was most unfortunate to Minta, for the so-called

Dr. Links was a villainous quack and he bound up Minta's beautiful face in a bungling manner, and as a result when the time came for the bones to be knit together, and the bandages removed, it was found that her lower jaw was askew, projecting her lip and jaw to one side in a startling manner to behold, changing the aspect of her countenance, maiming her, as it seemed, for life, and robbing her comely face of its beauty and attractiveness, for her face now conveyed no idea of the fine mental qualities she possessed, nor of the fine and tender feelings of her heart. While her mother felt deeply the calamity of this misfortune to her daughter, and gave to her a sympathy she had long ago withheld, her cynical husband viewed Minta's misfortune with unconcern and ridicule, and opposed his wife's pleadings to have the bone reset, but finally, after much urging, he reluctantly consented to have it done, but upon consulting a surgeon they were told that owing to the complicated nature of the fracture, and of its close proximity to the head and throat, that the result of such a course would be uncertain, owing to the difficulty of renewing the original fracture.

The purpose was then abandoned, and poor Minta seemed destined to carry this misfortune through life to her grave.

She resigned herself to this new affliction and bore it with fortitude, but did not abandon the resolution of improving her mind by some unknown, hoped-for means. But "where there is a will there is a way," and genius and perseverance will often accomplish unexpected results, and the want of means and opportunity, of which so many complain as a hindrance to their advancement, have, on the contrary, been the stepping stones to the grand achievements of others. Thus the early poverty of John Jacob Astor, Stephen Girard, A. T. Stewart and others taught them the great lesson of economy, by means of which they built vast fortunes, for "economy is wealth." The early poverty of Horace Greeley, Presidents Lincoln and Johnson, and others, was also the stepping stone to their greatness for they thereby were taught the value of time and how to use it judiciously. And thus Minta felt that she was destined in some unforeseen way to accomplish her noble purpose.

Having recovered sufficiently from her fall she again began her labours as a cowboy, which consisted in keeping the cattle together on the best grass and driving them to water at noon and home at night. It was not the labour in itself which made it an unpleasant task, but it was being alone all day, on the treeless, dry, sunny prairie, away from all that was pleasing to her. But to Minta this was not so great a deprivation after all, for her home was no longer pleasant to her, and it was a relief to her to be away from the reproaches and abuse ever heaped upon her. But Minta found a friend at last in her great need.

Mr. Heisel and family, a well-to-do stock-grower, settled in an adjacent valley, five miles from the McBrides, and in the vicinity of Minta's herding grounds. As Minta often called at the Heisel ranch for a drink of cool water, she thus became acquainted, and received much sympathy and kindness from Mrs. Heisel, who was a woman of culture and refinement, having been a "school-marm" before her marriage. She had a large library, a piano and other appurtenances of a well-furnished home, Minta timidly asked her for the loan of a book, which she freely granted, saying, "You can have others, also."

Thus was Minta made happy by the kindness of a friend, and ever after this when herding the cattle was she seen with book in hand, reading under the shadow of an improvised screen made of her blanket.

As the cows could be left alone for three or four hours at a time each day, Minta had ample time to visit Mrs. Heisel, who became to her a benefactor and a friend. She taught her to do fancy work, for which her genius and taste gave her an aptitude. Mrs. Heisel found a real pleasure in this benevolent work, for Minta had told her the sad history of her life in such beautiful and masterly language that she was prepossessed in her favour, and therefore willingly aided her in her praiseworthy effort. It was thus that Minta spent the eleventh and twelfth years of her life,, making the most of the poor opportunities she had for mental culture and improvement, for there were then no schools in cattle growing districts. But during the winter in which she had entered into her thirteenth year Ezra McBride had grown, occasionally, so ill natured to Minta that he often in his anger threatened to drive her away from home, and so deep and strong was his prejudice against her that he seemed to be pleased when she was out of his sight.

Her mother, seeing the condition of affairs, and for the peace and quiet of the family, and for the advantage of Minta, was considering where to find her a more pleasant home.

While matters thus stood Mrs. Heisel called upon the McBrides to ascertain if she could secure the services of Minta for a few weeks. She was surprised to learn that her parents would permit Minta to go for an unlimited time, simply for her board and clothing and three months' tuition in the year. Thus Minta's home was now changed to Heisel's, which filled her with delight—for it was a happy change to her. All was now so pleasant and genial to her that she seemed to have been transported into another and a happier world.

During the early part of the first summer of her residence with the Heisels she met with an accident which nearly cost her her life. She was thrown violently to the ground from a horse which she was riding, knocking her senseless and severely injuring her about the head. When she had come to her senses again it was found that her jaw was once more broken. A good surgeon was secured, and when it was healed and the bandages removed her jaw was luckily natural and straight again, her teeth and lips meeting, properly, which again changed her features, this time for the better, rendering her once more beautiful and attractive, much to the delight of Mrs. Heisel.

In the autumn of that year, and on the twenty-fifth day of September, the Colorado Agricultural Fair was to be held in Denver, and a premium purse of three hundred dollars in gold, donated by a rich mining man, was to be awarded to the best young lady rider, none but misses over the age of twelve and not over sixteen years to compete. Minta, now in her thirteenth year, desired to compete for this prize. Mrs. Heisel made over for Minta one of her gayest riding habits and Minta was furnished a beautiful black horse upon which she trained for the contest. When the day arrived Minta was on hand, anxious and excited, and as beautiful in her gay dress as a full blown rose. With the assistance of Mr. Heisel, at the appointed time she appeared mounted on her noble black horse in lady-like posture, and without a saddle, being seated on a single red blanket folded and held to place by a surcingle. Many pioneers of the early days of Colorado will remember the excitement of the vast crowd of spectators on this occasion. As the competitors, six in number, leisurely walked their horses around the race track, some said of Minta: "Doesn't she look well." Others, "I wonder how she can stick on her horse without a side-saddle." Others said: "I bet she'll win."

All was now anxiety and excitement. The horses now increased their speed into a gentle trot, and as the contestants rode abreast, it was a grand and beautiful sight to behold these young and fair contestants. As they increased their speed the crowd gave forth loud shouts of encouragement. When the excitement was at its height and the horses were in a lope, Minta, affected by the exciting influences around her, the brass band, with its stimulating music, the applauding shouts of the people, had her spirits so aroused that she leaped to her feet, and standing on her horse, thus rode around the half-mile track, amid the deafening shouts of the people. She then gracefully dropped to her former position on the back of her horse. It was not hard to predict who had won the prize. Within an hour's time Minta was informed that the judges had awarded the prize to her. Thus was she in a measure compensated for her services as a "cowboy," by which she had gained the skill that won her the purse of gold. And thus what seemed once the most hopeless conditions for her advancement was the very means by which it was attained, for this money enabled her to begin her education.

Mr. Heisel, having sold out his large herd of cattle and ranch for a princely sum, now made his abode with his family in his stylish brick residence on a fashionable street in the gay and bustling city of Denver. Minta now had all the advantages of a stylish and comfortable home and the benefits of the best society secured to her. By this happy turn of fortune in her favour she was enabled to obtain several years' tuition at the Denver University, an institution of learning equal to any for boys and girls, with but a small outlay of money. By advice of Mr. Heisel and a wide-awake real estate agent, she placed fifty dollars in a rough looking lot on a back street. This investment proved fortunate for her, for the incomprehensible and wondrous growth of the Queen City of the Plains soon spread around and beyond it, in the short time of three years, so as to increase its value more than a hundred fold. But Minta did not sell it, for she was still a pupil at school, as eager as ever to store her mind with useful knowledge, and she was not led away from her course nor bewildered by the dazzling prospect of her good fortune. But her last year at school was now, drawing to a close, and the "commencement exercises," so-called, would close her career as a school girl. She was allowed by her teachers, as a courtesy, and in recognition of her great literary attainment, to select her own subject for an original address, and on the program appeared her name thus: "Valedictorian, Minta Abel."

A large crowd of people filled the University Hall on this occasion, and when Minta appeared on the platform, and looked over the audience with that leisure and quiet, indicative of self reliance and ability, anxiety and interest was manifested in every face; for the magnetic power of her presence was felt by all. The figure she presented as she thus stood was grand in the extreme, and one which many a more tenderly raised young lady would envy. Her beautiful face was flushed with the glow of good health, and every feature bore marks of intellectual superiority.

She possessed a form of such lithesome grace, and beauty of proportions, as is only obtained by outdoor life and exercise. Her voice was full and melodious, her words sprang from her lips as clear and distinct as sounds from a bell. She spoke more as an accomplished orator than as a school girl. She spoke without the conventional manuscript, and, as it were, from the impulse of the moment. A breathless silence reigned throughout the hall, as she became earnest in her discourse, and when she began to describe the duties of the pupils when they entered upon the realities of life, the buffets, the malice and selfishness of the world, and of the fortitude and moral integrity requisite to offset this, she spoke with such eloquence and power, and with such an easy flow of words, that she surprised and fascinated all with the grandeur, logic and beauty of her address.

After leaving school she was urged by admiring friends to study law in emulation of Mrs. Clara Foltz, the phenomenal and successful woman lawyer of San Francisco, Cal. She readily formed this resolution, and to that end had sold her city lot for the snug sum of six thousand dollars. But, on the eve of her departure for the law school, she learned from a friend that her cruel stepfather was deeply in debt, owing to his bad management of her mother's affairs, and that he and her mother would lose their home in consequence of the foreclosure of a mortgage. Her mind was made up in an instant.

The sale of the McBride homestead was the occasion for the gathering together of a large crowd of queerly dressed cowboys and ranchmen. Before the auctioneer began the sale, a well dressed lady, an apparent stranger to all, drove up in a gay livery rig, and attracted the attention of all for a while. She looked upon the scene with apparent unconcern till the sale began, when she drove closer to the auctioneer. When apparently the last bid, fifteen hundred dollars, was made and the warning given that the sale would soon close for want of bids, sixteen hundred dollars was heard to come from the solitary lady in the carriage. All eyes were then directed towards her, while wonder filled the minds of all present, and Mr. and Mrs. McBride, who looked sorrowfully upon the sad scene, wondered more than all others. Sixteen hundred and fifty dollars came from a bystander. Seventeen hundred dollars was offered. Eighteen hundred dollars from the lady in the carriage. This was the last bid and the sale was closed.

She now hitched her team to the fence with the skill of an adept, and with the fortitude of a soldier entered the house she had left five years before, and in a haughty tone and manner said to her cruel stepfather:

"Ezra McBride, this is the day of my triumph and the

day you shall be humiliated for the cruelty you unjustly and heartlessly heaped upon me when a child under this very roof."

"That's false, you never wus under this here roof afore," said he, hissing the words through the space of his tooth.

"Do you know Minta Abel, whom you drove from this house," she replied, "and who now enters by right of law, and who may or may not treat you in a like cruel manner?"

Ezra McBride now recognizing Minta, cried out in an agony of grief: "Oh, Minta, furgive, furgive me," and he wept like a child. Her mother, bewildered, confused and sad, asked her forgiveness, and also wept, while Nana, her little half sister, looked on in sad wonder.

After the needed explanations were made by each, and her father had apologized for his cruel, ungovernable temper, a better feeling took possession of all, and Minta then made out a free life lease of the ranch to her father and mother.

After an affectionate parting with them she rode away and entered an eastern law school, from which in due time she graduated. She then took up her abode in Helena, Montana, where she opened a law office on one of its busy streets, and she has now, it is reported, already secured a lucrative law practice in both the upper and lower courts.

Thus we see that success in life depends more upon determined effort, unyielding perseverance and industry than upon great advantages or upon ample means, as exemplified in this sketch of the life of the "Cow Herder Girl."

*9 7 8 1 8 4 6 7 7 7 4 7 9 *